These Might Help Too

Homilies for Cycle C

✠ Joseph Cassidy

VERITAS

Published 2006 by
Veritas Publications
7/8 Lower Abbey Street
Dublin 1
Ireland
Email publications@veritas.ie
Website www.veritas.ie

ISBN 1 85390 989 0
978 1 85390 989 4 (from January 2007)

Scripture quotations taken from *The New Revised Standard Version Bible*
© 1993 and 1998 by the Division of Christian Education of the National
Council of the Churches of Christ in the United States of America.

Designed by Colette Dower
Printed in the Republic of Ireland by Betaprint, Dublin

*Veritas books are printed on paper made from the wood pulp of managed
forests. For every tree felled, at least one tree is planted, thereby renewing
natural resources.*

I dedicate these homilies to the parishioners of
Moore and Clonfad who were the first to hear them
and who are producing much better homilies
in their own lives.

Contents

Introduction

As every preacher knows, there are seven days in every week and at least one homily. No matter what our other commitments may be in the course of a week, the homily will have to be done. Sometimes we are so pressed for time (or so accustomed to the leisurely run of it) that we cannot find it within ourselves to prepare a homily at all. Although we are very conscious of the privilege involved in preaching and the opportunity that is ours, the homily over the years so plunders our resources and makes such incessant demands that we wouldn't be human if now and again we weren't tempted to 'give up the ghost'. So on rare occasions (I hope) we go to the files rather than the sources. We produce something for consumption that has been produced at least once before. 'They'll never notice the difference', we tell ourselves reassuringly, knowing in our hearts that even if they don't, we will. We will know it in the feeling that isn't there, the staleness of the experience, the deadness of the delivery. Most of all, we'll know it in the betrayal of the moment – the God-given opportunity that we've allowed to slip by. Old songs may be sung again and old poems recited. But old homilies have only a mayfly existence, except on the written page.

Three years pass more quickly in the life of a preacher than in the life of anybody else. Or so it seems. Before we know where we are, before you could say A, B, C, the same three readings come around to us again. We address ourselves to the challenge they represent at a different time and in a different context. They will make fresh demands on us now perhaps – the breaking of new ground that we hadn't even trodden on before. Whatever we come up with, under the guidance of the Spirit, should be essentially our own. All our homilies, in human terms, must be of our own making. But others can play a part. They can be part of the mix – give us an idea, make a present of a phrase, suggest an approach, get the process in motion. If *These Might Help*, published six years ago, has a role to play in that process, then it is my fervent hope that there might be a similar role for *These Might Help Too*. And I would hope as well that this new collection of homilies or reflections would have the same appeal for the general public as did the old.

Finally, I wish to thank Veritas (and editor Caitriona Clarke in particular) for the personal kindness shown and the professional help given to me in the preparation of this publication. I thank the people of Moore and Clonfad in whose faithful presence these homilies were 'tested' for the first (and last) time. Nobody has worked with me on this project with greater kindness or constancy than my secretary, Ms Mary Phelan. I say a special 'thank you' to her for all her help.

✠ Joseph Cassidy
Moore
September 2006

Season

of

Advent

A Stirring of Conscience

Jer 33:14-16; 1 Thess 3:12–4:2; Lk 21:25-28, 34-36

This is the first Sunday of Advent and it should be the beginning of something for all of us. It's the beginning of something already in that it's the first day of the Church's year, but because it doesn't coincide with what we call the New Year, it doesn't make much of an impact. Nobody was up last night ringing out the old year – except those who were going to be up anyway. Nobody will say to you this morning, 'Happy New Year'. If there are those who do, you'll be looking at them!

The danger of all this is that we'd take no notice of Advent at all, that we'd leave it to itself to gather its own momentum. Give it a name and leave it alone. Give it a nod but no acknowledgement. But that's not the way we should treat it at all. When morning comes, we prepare for the day. When Advent comes we prepare for our Saviour. Jeremiah reminds us of his coming in today's first reading. 'I will make a virtuous branch grow for David, who shall practise honesty and integrity in the land. In those days Judah shall be saved and Israel shall dwell in confidence' (Jer 33:15). The 'virtuous branch' about whom Jeremiah makes his prophecy is Jesus himself (Jer 25:3-6).

The bird that's most associated with Christmas is the unfortunate turkey – but Christmas is not all about turkeys, or Brussels sprouts either, tasty and all as these may be. What Christmas is about essentially is the birth of our Saviour, which is a profoundly spiritual event, and because that is the case, our preparation for it should be profoundly spiritual too. So we'll post the cards, write the letters, send the emails, make the phone calls – that's fine. We'll exchange the gifts, remember our friends, celebrate with our relations, have our family feast. That's fine too – all part of our humanity and our spirituality as well because the human and the spiritual are inextricably intertwined. All I'm saying is that there is another level of spirituality that could be left untroubled underground, and were that to be left untroubled we would not be preparing for a Saviour. For a feast, yes. For a Saviour, no!

What's this other level of spirituality that could be left untroubled underground? Well, there are some clear references to it in the second reading and the Gospel – both of which refer, not to our Lord's first coming at Christmas, but to his Second Coming in judgement. Paul prays in the second reading that the Lord will increase 'our love for one another and the whole human race' (1 Thess 3:12). He prays that we'll be found blameless in the sight of God, 'when the Lord comes with all his saints' (1 Thess 3:13). Jesus warns us to be careful lest our lives be 'coarsened by debauchery and drunkenness' and urges us to 'pray at all times for the strength to survive … and to stand with confidence before the Son of Man' (Lk 21:34-36). Both of them are taking the long view. Neither of them is thinking of Christmas. Advent is only partly about its public self – about short-term preparation for Christmas. It's also about life – long preparation for the Second Coming of Christ.

What we need to ensure this Advent is that when Christmas Day is over there will be more than a carcass left. There will be a spiritual legacy left, please God, a renewed commitment to the prayerful and virtuous life outlined for us in today's readings. Love of others; blamelessness in the sight of God; freedom from debauchery and drunkenness; prayerfulness. Let's reflect on these in turn for a moment! Are we as loving as Christians as we ought to be? Is there no room for improvement there? Nobody that we have overlooked or ignored or treated badly? Nobody that we deliberately exclude? In that respect and in all others are we 'blameless in the sight of our God' (1 Thess 3:13)? And if

THESE MIGHT HELP TOO

our hearts are not 'coarsened with debauchery and drunkenness' (Lk 21:34), and it's quite possible that they are, surely there must be something in our way of life that is out of step with the Gospel? We can be so perceptive about other people – their faults and shortcomings – and so deluded about ourselves. Delightedly deluded sometimes! Maybe the first thing we need to pray for this Advent is spiritual insight. And after that, the courage to change. When things remain the same in our lives, when sinfulness continues to prevail, it is because we have allowed Christ to recede into the background and the light of conscience to grow dim. We have chosen to live in the sinful now, where morality can be kept at bay. If beneath the hustle and bustle that heralds the coming of Christmas we have this stirring of conscience in lives that are stalling, then Advent will have really begun.

John the Baptist

Bar 5:1-9; Phil 1:3-6, 8-11; Lk 3:1-6

Did you notice the build up in today's Gospel? A bit like the rolling of drums or a flourish of trumpets! The roll call of historic names – Herod, Pilate, Philip, Lysanias, Annas, Caiphas, coming to a resounding climax with the name of John the Baptist. An awful lot of Advent belongs to John the Baptist. He'll turn up next Sunday in the Gospel. He'll turn up again the Sunday after that. He's a booming presence in the Gospel of today. Is he making too much of himself? No, he's not! We, on our part, may be making too little of him.

John the Baptist is a major figure in human history for at least three reasons. The first is that the story of Jesus in the Gospel begins with him. He was the one chosen by God to prepare the way for his Son. He didn't just happen to be there. He was meant to be there. In God's plan, he was God's man! God was very particular in the Immaculate Conception about choosing a mother for his Son. He was also very particular about the prophet who would be his precursor. John the Baptist was handpicked – one of a very privileged number who was headhunted from heaven. Secondly, John is a major figure in that he not only prepared an audience for Jesus, he also prepared an elite. He prepared a group of disciples who would be key people in Christ's kingdom. One was Peter; another was Andrew; a third was John the Evangelist. John the Baptist gathered them around himself and then let them go – encouraged them to go! Did you know that? That some of our Lord's best disciples were John's disciples first? The third reason as to why John is a major figure is that he was intimately linked with Christ in time and in relationship. He wasn't a voice from the past – he was an endorsement of Christ in

16   THESE MIGHT HELP TOO

the present. His was a contemporary voice, powerful in its own right, persuasive because of its own resonance, but muted in his role as precursor. 'I baptise you in water for repentance, but the one who follows me is more powerful than I am, and I am not fit to carry his sandals; he will baptise you with the Holy Spirit and fire' (Mt 3:15-16). In the relay of life, if you like, he ran the penultimate leg, passed on the baton and willed Christ to the finish. He was great in his humility and would prove even greater in his martyrdom. Jesus himself had no doubt about the stature of the Baptist in history. 'I tell you solemnly, of all the children born of women, a greater than John the Baptist has never been seen' (Mt 11:11).

So John the Baptist deserves our attention. His words should carry weight. 'Prepare a way for the Lord. Make his paths straight' (Mt 3:3). At this time of year we find ourselves preparing for a feast. He wants us to prepare for a person. Although Christmas is a feast that carries Christ's name and celebrates his birth, preparation for it has become so frenetic in our culture that it can easily distract us from himself. John the Baptist is not distracted at all. The commentators would describe him as very focussed. God is on his way in the person of the Messiah. That's his message for us. It's a wonderfully joyous occasion in that 'All mankind shall see the salvation of God' (Lk 3:6), but it is an immensely challenging time as well. The challenge it represents is the challenge to conversion. And conversion itself is a root and branch affair, requiring such a radical internal change that our external behaviour becomes completely different. He gives a few examples in next Sunday's Gospel of what he has in mind. The person with 'two tunics must share with the man who has none and the one with something to eat must do the same' (Lk 3:11). Tax collectors must exact no more than their rate while soldiers must no longer intimidate (Lk 3:14). When John talks about 'making paths straight', 'filling valleys in', 'making rough ways smooth', he's talking about a spiritual revolution. He's talking about moral rather than physical obstacles to advancement (Lk 3:4-5). He is thinking about how resistant we all are to internal change. Old habits make good roadblocks. Old attitudes are formidable obstructions. Old sins are the biggest boulders of all. Either we change for Christ's coming or we don't. Either we'll open our hearts to him or we won't. Minds have to be made up, John is saying. Choices have to be made and axes are there to help us. 'Even now the axe is laid to the roots of the tree, so that any tree which fails to produce good fruit will be cut down and thrown on the fire' (Lk 3:9). He's a pretty insistent prophet, this John the Baptist. He has a pertinent question for all of us. We're lucky he's not here in person to put it to us. His question is: 'Where does Christ fit into your Christmas?'

Keeping Christ in Christmas

Zeph 3:14-18; Phil 4:4-7; Lk 3:10-18

A few years ago, I asked a friend of mine, an old man, what Christmas was like when he was young. He came from a small farm near my home place – from a countryside that was a patchwork of small farms, of chimney-puffing thatched houses and walled-in handkerchiefs of land. What kind of a celebration did ye have, I said to him? Well, he said, we'd pull the table out from under the window into the middle of the kitchen floor. We'd all sit around it, and for the supper on Christmas Eve we'd have a bit of a herring and jam. Not a full herring mind you, a bit of a one, and a pound pot of jam. And what about Christmas Day, I asked. Oh, Christmas Day would be the usual, he told me, nothing extra. An odd year, a neighbour might come with a small drop of whiskey in a bottle and the old folk would sit around the fire after dinner and drink a drop of punch. He said nothing about Santa. I presume that if Santa did come, he left no trace. Another man from that part of the country told me that in the days before Christmas, the people would be in lines along the stone walls outside the local post office waiting for the letter from America. If the letter didn't come, they'd have no Christmas at all.

That kind of Christmas experienced by these people is euros away from our world. And what has made the difference in our case is, of course, affluence. We are much better off nowadays than ever we were before.

Whereas in the old days even the relatively affluent could bring the Christmas home in an ass-cart in a while of.a day, what you see now in supermarkets is lines and lines of trolleys heaped up with Christmas like the horse-carts heaped up with turf in days gone by. In several fundamental ways, affluence has made it easier for us. And we have to regard that as a blessing. The herring and jam days are gone, for most people anyway, and nobody wants them back.

At the same time, affluence has brought its own problems, especially in terms of expense and pressure. And for that reason alone some people have come to hate Christmas. It's such a consumerist time of year now, such a consumerist binge, such an elbowing experience, that it has to be endured rather than enjoyed. What people hate is the hassle. The cards, the gifts, the queues, the cost and the expensive expectations the children have of Santa. It's a race against time now as well, a feast that has become more and more a deadline. 'We'll have to get it done before Christmas.' There is so much to be done before Christmas that most of us are 'done in' when it arrives.

And then, on this particular Sunday, the third Sunday of Advent, with the pressure on the increase, the Church tells us to 'rejoice'. 'Rejoice, rejoice,' she says, and we think to ourselves, 'they must be in another world'! And in a sense they are. You see, Christmas is a global feast – a cosmic feast. It is celebrated against a variety of backgrounds. Not just against our background. It has the whole wide world as its backdrop. It will be celebrated in many other countries as indulgently as in our own.

　　　　　　　　THESE MIGHT HELP TOO

But there are other places where the past is alive and well – where herring and jam would be a luxury. There are places ravaged by war where to be in uniform or just an innocent civilian is an enormous risk. Or there is a vast tract of Africa where death stalks the land, where Aids devours and destroys. So the Church is saying to us 'rejoice', not because our trolley is full – though that's fine if it happens – but because with the coming of Christ our life is full of meaning, as is the life of those who will have to struggle through Christmas with empty trolleys, in poverty or sickness or war. It is not the circumstances of our lives that make Christmas. What makes Christmas is the birth of Jesus Christ. And that is the heart of the matter. The point of the whole thing.

And it's the birth of Christ – the coming of Christ – that's invoked and celebrated all through today's mass. 'Yahweh your God is in your midst,' the first reading tells us. 'He will renew you by his love' (Zeph 3:17). 'The Lord is my strength and my song,' Isaiah tells us in the psalm. 'He became my Saviour' (Is 12:2). 'I want you to be happy,' St Paul tells us in the second reading, because 'the Lord is very near' (Phil 4:4, 5). A feeling of expectancy had grown amongst the people, the Gospel tells us, because they were beginning to think that John the Baptist might be the Christ (Lk 4:15). It was the Christ that the people wanted. The Christ they needed. The Christ we all need. In one sentence, my dear people, Christmasses come and go – whether we like them or not – but Christ goes on forever. His teaching does, his love for us does, his salvation does. He's the key to our year. The key to our lives! We have to make him the key to our Christmas in the way we love each other, repent of our sins and confess them and in the way we receive him in the Holy Eucharist. The commercial skin on Christmas is fine, provided we have a spiritual core. I have here one of the cards I got for Christmas. It says simply, 'No greater King was ever born. No greater life has ever been. No greater love could ever be'. Unless he is the centre of our Christmas celebration, then it is not really Christmas at all.

A New Baby

Mic 5:2-5; Heb 10:5-10; Lk 1:39-45

They were carrying his mother out the back door to a hackney car – the driver, the local doctor and his own father. The young lad was very puzzled and a bit shocked. They were going to a place in Dublin called the 'Rotunda' to get a new baby. They had never got babies in Dublin before. The nurse had always come to the house, asked for soap, a towel and a basin of hot water and got a new baby somewhere upstairs. It didn't make sense to a six year old boy, in the late 1930s, to go all the way to Dublin (132 miles in fact), over narrow bumpy roads, in a cold car, to get a new baby. And especially a Dublin one! Besides, his mother didn't look well enough to be out searching for a baby. The older people weren't behaving as they normally would. There must be something wrong.

There was indeed. The sense of unease grew among all the children when the neighbours moved in to take care of them while their parents were away. They were terrified for their mother in case she'd never come back. It was a comfort and yet a worry that the doctor and nurse had travelled with her. The goodness in the adult world kept their anxiety from spilling over while they waited for news from Dublin. For days there was no word at all. They had rolled up their jackets, left them down as goalposts on the main street of the town, where only the occasional bicycle passed by, when word came from the post office that Mammy and Daddy had got a baby girl somewhere in the Rotunda. The moment was bathed in sunlight. They stood there in the street, letting the blessing sink in, noticing the blueness of the sky, the football forgotten. Their mother would come home again. She had survived whatever sickness had come over her. And the baby she'd bring with her would be (as it turned out) a source of great warmth and joy.

There is a story behind every birth, especially for the mother. For that reason, among others, on this last Sunday of Advent, on the eve of our Lord's birthday, the Church focuses on Mary. As far as we know, her life wasn't particularly at risk, as was the life of my mother in that little story I've just told you. But bringing a baby into the world was a risky business in the harsh conditions of her time. Palestine was a disease-ridden place. The number of people who presented themselves to Jesus for healing indicates very strongly that such was the case. The life span for humans had to be short. The number of mothers and babies who died in childbirth must have been very high. Mary and Joseph were poor people. When they presented the child Jesus in the temple, for instance, they did so with the offering of the poor, a pair of turtle doves (Lk 2:24). The poverty they experienced themselves and the impoverished conditions around them would have increased their vulnerability and made their lives that bit more precarious. The journey to Elizabeth that Mary undertook during her pregnancy, in primitive conditions, must have been very hard on her. It was a four-day caravan journey through hilly country which, even with a rest in between, meant an eight day trek in all. In addition to physical hardship like that, every expectant mother is bound to be anxious about the birth of her baby. Her biggest concerns are that the baby will be healthy and that she herself will survive. Those concerns had to be in Mary's mind as well. They would have been particularly acute in the hazardous conditions that prevailed. It must be acknowledged, of course, that knowing what she did about the parentage of her child, Mary must have been greatly reassured in the knowledge that God was with her. But she must also have been conscious of a responsibility that was particular to herself.

How much all that reduced or added to the normal anxieties that pregnancy brings with it, we will never know. I mentioned earlier that Mary's life was at no particular risk before Jesus was born, but she did have another long journey to make from Nazareth to Bethlehem on the hackney car of the time, the serviceable if slow-moving donkey. There were no doctors or nurses to travel with her either and no guarantee of a bed for her delivery at journey's end. There was no Rotunda in Bethlehem. In fact, as they were to discover, not to their great surprise I imagine, 'there was no room for them at the inn' (Lk 2:7). The statues we see of Mary cannot be other than statuesque. They remind us of her existence but make us forget her humanity. This Sunday helps to underline her humanity. It helps to situate her positively and realistically within the glorious morass that is the human condition. As well as that, if her family in Nazareth could have got a phone call from Bethlehem to let them know that Jesus was born and Mary was safe, they'd have stopped whatever they were doing, let the blessing sink in and noticed the blueness in the sky. And they'd discover when she'd bring the baby home – as in fact they did discover – that he would be a source of great warmth and joy in their lives. Far more than that, they would discover that this child was the Messiah they had all been waiting for, the one who would 'stand and feed his flock with the power of Yahweh, with the majesty of the name of his God' (Mic 5:3, 4). He would be for all of them much more than a source of warmth and joy, someone who would enrich their lives at the human level. He would do that surely. But he would also bridge the gap for them between earth and heaven. He would, as unifier of people and reconciler with God, fulfil the prophecy of Micah in today's first reading when he said, 'He himself will be peace' (Mic 5:5).

Season

of

Christmas

Immortal Diamond

Is 9:1-7; Titus 2:11-14; Lk 2:1-14
(Midnight Mass)

I hope there is not a child in the parish who doesn't love Christmas because Christmas for a child is the world before the fall, a winter paradise where innocence and goodness reign supreme. Christmas for children is an experience of glitter and magic that will lodge in the memory for the rest of their lives.

Not every adult feels the same. Innocence doesn't last forever. Some people tell me that they hate Christmas. I have to say that, although there's a lot of hassle in the run-up to it, and an inevitable loneliness at the heart of it, I like it very much. I like it because in the winter cold, people generate their own warmth. It's a kind of substitute for the summer sun. I love the rise in human temperature, the kindness that people show, the annual surfacing of friendship that is submerged throughout the year. Christmas jogs our memories in a way that other feasts do not. Among the cards I received last Christmas, two were different. One was unsigned; it simply said, 'Thanks very much' – enclosed a gift and left no name! Christmas celebrated anonymously, which was lovely. There was nothing written in the second card at all. Well intentioned but badly directed. And yet there are two people out there who helped to make my Christmas anyway. Signed no name but left their mark.

Another side of Christmas that I like very much is getting in touch with the family. Those of us whose families have scattered can be out of contact for much of the year. To some extent we are all prisoners of our own place – captives of our own commitments. But at Christmas, flesh and blood reasserts itself. We make a special effort – as members of the same family and as inheritors of Christmas past – to show affection to our own, to be reunited with our own, if at all possible. On Christmas day I go to members of my family in Athlone. And when I'm travelling there, one of the things I love is the quietness on the roads. The feeling that people have abandoned the rush and gone back to their roots. The traffic defers to the family. The wheel gives way to the circle – the family circle. It's a day for priorities, a day for home.

The third thing I like about Christmas is the light it throws on the human condition and the sense it inserts into my own life. We are all running out of Christmasses and the people who made Christmas for me and mine when we were children are long since dead. But they are not dead in my heart, or in my memory. But living on in my memory won't immortalise them. It won't make them last forever. What will make them last forever is that they are alive in the memory and heart of God. The readings in tonight's mass assure me that they are. 'The people that walked in darkness,' the first reading tells me, 'have seen a great light' (Is 9:2). 'For there is a child born for us, a son given to us' (Is 9:5-6). St Paul tells us in the second reading that 'God's grace has been revealed and it has made salvation possible for the whole human race' (Titus 2:11). St Luke couldn't make it any plainer than when he says: 'Today in the town of David, a Saviour has been born to you; he is Christ the Lord' (Lk 2:11).

I have just been reading of a life of Gerard Manley Hopkins. He was a convert to Catholicism, became a Jesuit priest and later earned renown as one of the most distinctive poetic voices of the nineteenth century. He captures the mood of Christmas in one of his letters in a few lovely phrases. He describes it as having 'a topsy turvy, cheerful air' and then he goes on, 'Christmas is being hung everywhere'. He tried to capture the meaning of Christmas too but that didn't come as easily to him because he

THESE MIGHT HELP TOO

suffered from bouts of deep depression. He was in such mental turmoil at times that he described the mind as having 'mountains' – mountains to climb and heights from which to fall. 'O the mind,' he said, 'the mind has mountains; cliffs of fall, frightful, sheer, no-man-fathomed!'[1] He wrote on one occasion that Our Lady and St Joseph found comfort from coldness (of all kinds) on Christmas night and that 'their comfort was Christ's birth'.[2] There was great comfort in that for Hopkins too, because Christ's birth would lead to Resurrection, not just for Christ himself but for the rest of us as well.

> In a flash, at a trumpet crash,
> I am all at once what Christ is, since he was what I am, and
> This Jack, joke, poor potsherd, patch, matchwood, immortal diamond,
> Is immortal diamond.[3]

So if 'immortal diamond' is what we are because of Christ's birth, death and resurrection then it seems we are not running out of Christmasses at all. That's the great thing. And won't there be a great quietness on the roads when all of us have finally gone home?

Notes

1. 'No worst, there is none' from *Hopkins, A Literary Biography*, by Norman White, Clarendon Press, 1992.
2. Ibid., 'Spiritual Diary'.
3. Ibid., 'That Nature is a Heraclitean Fire and Of the Comfort of the Resurrection'.

Light the Candles

Is 9:1-7; Titus 2:11-14; Lk 2:1-14
(Midnight Mass)

This year for the first time in my life, I found myself resenting Christmas. It came too soon for a start. Where the past year went, I don't know. Vapourised! Christmas is being hijacked anyway by powerful commercial forces in the interests of sales rather than salvation. The run-up to Christmas has become such a scramble and there is so much hassle involved that I said to myself, 'What I need now is a bypass'. A Christmas bypass. Some way of getting round it as if it weren't there at all. And we know from previous experience that as soon as the dinner is over, the bubble bursts. The turkey strikes back! I was going to put it in the newsletter that if anyone had an apartment or a villa in Spain or Morocco or someplace, then I'd be prepared to look after it for the next few weeks. I didn't do it, because you'll probably be going there yourself!

And then the first Christmas cards began to arrive and people are so kind to go to the trouble. We went collecting for Pakistan with the young people in the Ginger Group and the buckets were filling up with Christmas practicality. And then I came home one evening and there was a bottle of something leaning up against the front door. It lifted my heart because, just as one swallow doesn't make a summer, one bottle doesn't make the Christmas and there was always the prospect of a few bottles more! And then the crib was set up, and the children who came to 5.30 Mass with their parents this evening found Christmas magic in the crib as they always do. I thought to myself, even in this sophisticated age when we have access to the internet and things like that, there is still some kind of elemental message that comes only from a stable!

And then I found myself warming to Christmas again. And I recalled the story that the Cork writer Frank O'Connor recounted in his autobiography. He tells us that one Christmas when he was a little boy Santa brought him a toy engine. On Christmas day his mother brought him to visit the convent, where he saw the baby Jesus in the crib. He was very upset when he saw him because, little as he had himself, the baby Jesus had nothing at all. He had no toys. Frank put it down to the incompetence of Santa Claus. Then he said to one of the nuns, 'Does the baby Jesus not like toys?' And the nun said, 'Oh, he does – but his mother is too poor to buy them!' 'Well,' said O'Connor, 'that settled it. I climbed into the crib and I put the toy engine into the baby Jesus' outstretched arms. I probably showed him how to wind it too, because a little baby like that wouldn't know how. I remember the feeling of "reckless generosity" I had when I left him there in the darkness of the chapel clutching the toy engine to his chest!' O'Connor had given him all and he was happy.

Let me finish with the one little point I want to make. O'Connor thought he was giving a gift to the baby Jesus. And so he was! What he didn't fully realise as a young child was that the baby Jesus was God's gift to him and to all humankind. Something much more precious than a toy was being placed in his own little hands. He was being gifted himself without fully realising it. Christmas is about the love of God made visible in the body of a child. 'God loved the world so much that he gave his only Son so that everyone that believes in him may not be lost but may have eternal life' (Jn 3:16).

If we are going to talk about reckless generosity, then the most reckless generosity of all has come from above. The benevolence of earth is no match for the munificence of heaven. 'For there is a child born to us, a son given to us' (Is 9:5-6). That's what we are celebrating at Christmas. And no amount of commercialism can ever asphyxiate it. The

German theologian, Karl Rahner, put the point very well when he said:

> When we say it's Christmas
> We mean that God has spoken into the world,
> His last, his deepest, his most beautiful word ...
> And this word means 'I love you, I love you,
> The World and people'.[1]

To know that you are loved is one of the most wonderful knowings of all. Nothing sustains us in life like the guaranteed love of another. Just knowing that a person is there for us is an enormous enrichment and reassurance. What Christmas is telling us is that not only is God there for us, but that he is there for us all the time. He is never away; never too busy. We are never out of his mind, not even for an instant. This unwavering love of God for us is the most enduring Christmas present we could ever be given. And it is never in need of winding like O'Connor's Christmas toy. It is because God's love is so constant, so unconquerable and irrevocable that we have so much to celebrate at this time of year. God has given his all to us. The poet Robert Southwell put that well when he wrote, 'Gift better than himself God doth not know'. Needless to say we know no better gift either. 'Light the candles,' Rahner tells us. 'They have more right to exist than all the darkness.' Light the candles we will in humility and gratitude, and may we keep them lit, especially through the darkest hours as a constant reminder of the constancy of God.

Note
1.   Karl Rahner, *The Eternal Year*, Helicon, 1964.

God Made Man

Is 52:7-10; Heb 1:1-6; Jn 1: 1-18

What is the most unusual thing about the way we celebrate Christmas? I think it's that we celebrate it in suspense. By suspense I don't mean that we are waiting anxiously for something to happen. I mean that we stop what we are doing – we suspend what we are doing – because something has already happened to give us pause. The world pauses on Christmas Day – the Christian world anyway. It comes to a stand still, almost a complete standstill. And people, as external creatures, inhabitants of the marketplace, come to a standstill almost at the same time. They abandon the streets, keep only skeleton wheels revolving, retire to their homes, like denizens of the underground, snuggle closer to one another in awareness and giving, and then sit down together at roughly the same time to the same kind of dinner. Then, having been turkeyed, hammed, stuffed and suitably lubricated, they all recline on chairs and sofas, if there are enough chairs and sofas around, lapse into a slumberous condition, in so far as children will allow, and wake up again at roughly the same time and complain almost in unison, 'there's nothing on the television'. Why do people do this? It is the only time of year that we behave in such a predictably uniform way, that we leave the streets and offices to the luxury of their own oxygen. What a relief! Only something enormous – like the threat of a nuclear attack for instance – could make us take cover in this fashion. What happened in our history to make so many people behave like this – to precipitate this instinctive choreography? What kind of unearthly power has been vested in Christmas Day?

Some people would say that we behave the way we do for the obvious reason, that we are celebrating the birthday of a wonderful human being. And we can all subscribe to that. He has been such a presence in our lives, since we were children, that for twelve full days, beginning today, we make his birthday our own. There is nothing about Jesus that we cannot love: his devotion to the Father; his concern from the cross for his mother; his feeling for the sick; his identification with the poor; his understanding of sinners; his inclusion of outcasts; his forgiveness of enemies; his impatience with legalism and hypocrisy and the sheer scale and comprehensive of his love. The likes of him never walked the earth before and never will again. For his moral teaching alone he is held in the highest esteem. The author of the American Declaration of Independence, Thomas Jefferson, for instance, described the teachings of Jesus as 'the most benevolent and sublime probably that has ever been taught'. In 1941, Winston Churchill was discussing with a few friends how they might put the world together again after the war. 'The more closely we follow the Sermon on the Mount,' he said, 'the more likely we are to succeed in our endeavours'.[1] The simple peasants of Palestine who listened to Jesus with open mouths and expanding hearts paid him the highest tribute of all. They are the people on whose shoulders we stand. Speaking for myself, I love his stories that show his preference for the people who stray and overnight become the discards of society – the Prodigal Son, the Woman in Adultery, the Lost Sheep.

And yet, although he is a truly inspirational person and to my mind without equal in the history of humanity, he is not enough for me unless he is the Son of God. And I say that because those of us subject to sin and death need more than inspiration. We need salvation as well. To be taught on earth is fine. To be taken to heaven is final.

Is he the Son of God? Well, we meet two people in today's readings who are convinced that he is. One is John, who was his greatest friend. The other is Paul, who had been his greatest enemy. What John tells us is that 'the

THESE MIGHT HELP TOO

Word', the second person of the Trinity, 'was made flesh' (Jn 1:14). What Paul tells us is that 'at various times in the past … God spoke to our ancestors through the prophets, but in our own time … he has spoken to us through his Son (Heb 1:1-2). That Jesus is the Son of God and that he was made flesh as our Saviour is what Christmas is all about. If we make for our homes on Christmas day, it is because he made his home on earth. He came before we ran. What I call this 'instinctive choreography' has its origins in divinity. We leave the offices and streets, not just to their own oxygen but to ponder for a day or two the mystery of God made man and to listen for his footsteps on the sidewalks. We are celebrating today and for the next twelve days, not only because we are loved now but because we are destined to be loved eternally. In the knowledge of that love – and in the sharing of it together – let us all have a happy Christmas.

Note
1. E.P. Sanders, *The Historical Figure of Jesus*, Penguin, 1996, pp. 6–7.

The Dominance of Love

1 Sam 1:20-22, 24-28; 1 Jn 3:1-2, 2:21-24; Lk 2:41-52
or Eccles (Sir) 3:2-6, 12-14; Col 3:12-21; Lk 2:41-52

There is a huge portrait in Garbally College, Ballinasloe, of a Regent and later King of England called George IV (1762–1830). It has been there since the landlord days when the parent building in the College was owned by the Earls of Clancarty. George IV looks absolutely magnificent in this portrait. You look up at him and think, 'what an impressive man – so wonderfully handsome and resplendent'. He was handsome it seems, for a time, but in character and life style far from impressive. His tutor said of him when he was only fifteen years old that he'd 'either be the most polished gentleman or the most accomplished blackguard in Europe – possibly both'. He turned out to be a blackguard, 'a bad husband to his wife, a bad son to his father, a bad father to his son, a bad subject to his King, a bad King to his subjects'. The portrait in Garbally doesn't tell the full story. It is one-dimensional. It puts the emphasis on one aspect of the man only – his handsome appearance!

Just as that portrait misleads, a holy picture may mislead too. I'm thinking today of a picture of the Holy Family. There is so much emphasis on their holiness that you lose the sense of their humanity. You find yourself looking at three very special people, but so simplistically supernaturalised that it's very hard to identify with them at all. There they are up on the wall without seeming to have much contact with what's happening on the ground. Did our Lady ever smile? Did St Joseph ever get cross? Did Jesus get disconsolate or upset? I presume they did. They were all human. But what we get in holy pictures very often is fossilised serenity – a picture of people so permanently holy that they couldn't possibly be an example or a model for flesh and blood creatures like ourselves. If that's the conclusion we're inclined to come to, the fault is not in the Holy Family but in the one-dimensional manner in which it is so often portrayed.

One of the striking things about the Holy Family is that all through their lives they were beset with problems; not just the ordinary problems of making a living and putting bread on the table but much more difficult problems that were peculiar to themselves. Mary and Joseph, for instance, in their different ways were faced with a most perplexing pregnancy and in the rearing of the growing Jesus a most perplexing child. A child in the family couldn't be both human and divine without presenting the parents with the occasional conundrum. What, for instance, do you make of a young lad who, in losing himself for three days in Jerusalem, is really finding himself in the midst of 'the doctors, listening to them and asking them questions?' (Lk 2:46, 47). Before that kind of difficulty arose at all, how did Mary and Joseph cope with their fear for the safety of the baby Jesus and the hazards of their flight into Egypt? It was hard enough to find a place where he could be born. Now they had to find a place where he wouldn't be killed. The Holy Family didn't encounter the cross for the first time on Calvary. Although St Joseph wasn't to experience the ultimate horror of the crucifixion, the cross had been taking shape in all their lives over a number of years. If we are inclined to think of the Holy Family as serene and unassailable, then we have only to remember that it isn't in every family a son is hounded in his infancy and crucified in his prime. In the span of our Lord's life we see not just the happiness the family must have enjoyed but the suffering they endured as well.

One of the ways the Holy Family coped with their sufferings was to be there for one another. Not one of them was allowed to suffer alone. Joseph stood staunchly by Mary when lesser men might have turned her away. Mary stood steadfastly at the foot of the cross when some of the lesser men were already in flight. Jesus in his final agony was so worried and concerned about his mother that he entrusted the life-long care of her to the beloved St John. 'This is your mother' (Jn 19:27). Sometimes one gets the impression that the life of the Trinity can find human representation in the life of a family. We can certainly see the Trinitarian outline in the family from Nazareth. And what we are most conscious of as we reflect on the relationships within that family is the dominance and generosity of love.

That's the challenge thrown down to us today as family members – that all of us should become Trinitarians in the way that we love. And I know that, in most families, love is a constant thing throughout the year and a very costly thing at Christmas time. All of you parents will have done your best to make Christmas special for your children and they will have responded in kind. I know too that a family of its nature is an elastic entity, that it's sufficiently flexible to contain the arguments and disturbances that occur in families and that it can return in due course to its normal shape. What I do know too sadly is that some families are unhappier than they need be, because one member is more disruptive than the rest, because one member creates an atmosphere in which the others find it difficult to breathe. The source of the trouble may be a persistent silence or a degree of anger and intimidation that's almost a form of domestic terrorism. Without realising it fully, we can feed the desire to dominate and control. We can take advantage of gentleness. We can add to the sufferings of others who, in their own way, will have to suffer enough anyway. The fact of the matter is that the members of our family have only one life and we can make or break it. So let's please think about it, just in case. Let it be our primary objective to make the home for all the family a haven of peace. If I could give you a gift for the New Year, it would be a voucher for peace. It could be that somebody here is in a position to do that for your family. If that be the case, I pray from my heart that you'll give the voucher with the best of intentions and that God will help you to honour it faithfully in the years to come!

Caring for One Another

1 Sam 1:20-22, 24-28; 1 Jn 3:1-2, 2:21-24; Lk 2:41-52
or Eccles (Sir) 3:2-6, 12-14; Col 3:12-21; Lk 2:41-52

When I had finished in the National School long ago, I went on to St Nathy's in Ballaghadereen for post-primary education. It was a boarding school and in my experience a very good one. But in those days in boarding schools there were no weekend breaks, or even mid-term breaks. There were no breaks at all. Once you went in on 1 September you didn't put your nose out until the day before Christmas Eve. So it was prolonged incarceration – you were locked in for the whole term.

The holidays were great of course. We would be packing in our heads for months. The only thing about holidays is that they always come to an end. I hated going back to college, especially after Christmas. I hated leaving home, losing contact with my family and having to submit to the rigidity of an institutional regime. I used to go back on the bus very often and I'd pray on the way that the bus would crash. Now, I didn't want a bad crash. I didn't want anyone to be killed or anything. I didn't want to be killed myself either. I just wanted a broken leg or something – an accident that would keep me at home for the whole term with the leg up! That would have been my first choice. It never happened. God was big into boarding schools it seems; big into post-primary education.

Apart from having to go back, another regret I'd have would be the way I had behaved at home; if I was moodier, more short-tempered than I had intended to be, especially with my parents. Adolescence is a perplexing time for teenagers and parents alike and sometimes it can last for life.

Christmas is the one time of year when families make a point of getting together. It is prime time for families. And I

THESE MIGHT HELP TOO

hope that so far in your family everything has gone well. But as time goes on over a holiday, irritation can grow. People occupy one another's space, get in one another's way, get on one another's nerves. We all need family for the simple reason that we are family. It's the primary grouping to which we belong. We all need family for security and identity – to situate us in community. The forces that nurtured and shaped us in our youth and prepared us for the world never really let us go. By and large, we love going home, and home in turn welcomes us back. The unfortunate thing is that we can be less pleasant to members of our own family than to anybody else. Most of our charm is for external use only. It is spread very thinly indeed on home interiors. It takes a lot of polishing within the household to bring up a shine. I know we don't have to put on an act at home. But that doesn't mean we don't have to make an effort – and a recurring effort at that – to show kindness and consideration to the only people in the world who will really miss us when we die.

The Holy Family, whose feast we celebrate today, had many problems. The greatest period of tension, for instance, between Joseph and Mary had to be after their betrothal, when she was legally his wife and was found to be with a child that wasn't his. The hurt he must have experienced, the anger, and the confusion. He dealt with it! And although Jesus had to be an exceptionally fine character, he had to be for his father and mother, in his growing up, a most perplexing child. After all, although he was fully human, he was no ordinary mortal. They were puzzled, for example, and very upset when they lost him in Jerusalem at the age of twelve, and then, in the words of today's Gospel, 'found him in the Temple, sitting among the doctors, listening to them and asking them questions' (Lk 2:46, 47). Not the kind of thing you expect from your average twelve-year-old! As a couple, Joseph and Mary were uniquely gifted in their child but they were also uniquely challenged – an aspect of their lives together to which perhaps we don't give too much thought.

They rose to the challenge very well, and there is one way at least in which they can be a model for us and that's in the way they treated one another. Joseph was faithful to Mary and very protective of her even though the child born to Mary was not his own. Mary, as the instrument of God's will, was utterly devoted to her son, and summed up her entire attitude when she said to the waiters at Cana, 'Do whatever he tells you' (Jn 2:5). Jesus loved his mother so much and was so considerate of her that even when he was writhing in agony on the cross, one of the things that was uppermost in his mind was that John would look after her for the rest of her earthly life. God brought them together as a family but concern for one another kept them there. They grew in holiness together in the way that they loved.

So anyway, do your best in the situation in which you find yourself. And make the most of what's left of the Christmas holidays. If you have been home for the holiday and you are going back on the bus, I wouldn't expect you to be so lonely that you'd pray for it to crash! Just make sure that as you journey away from home there will be no room on your bus for regret!

Loving Mary

Num 6:22-27; Gal 4:4-7; Lk 2:16-21

One thing I can say in all honesty is that I love the Virgin Mary. It's an imperfect love, very often an impractical love, too often a purely sentimental love, but it's there. I love her like I love the fresh air or the green fields or the warmth of a fire. I love her because I can't help it. It's not something I decided, not something I arrived at. It's something that was decided for me, that came to me with my mother's milk. If you were to put me up against the wall and say 'Come on, be more specific, give me your reasons', I'd say 'Alright. If you insist, I'll try'. And I would start like this.

I love her for the obvious reason that she is Mother of God. *Theotokos. Muire.* Someone special. Let's put it at its most simplistic. Supposing I was a great friend of yours and I went to visit your house. And let's say that your mother was there and that I completely ignored her – was completely indifferent to her. You wouldn't like it. To ignore her is to ignore you. To love her is to love you. You cannot love Jesus without loving his mother. Love of Mary is an extension of our love of God. It is part of our faith, even at its most sophisticated, to be deeply, unashamedly, incurably tender towards Mary. And talking of 'incurably', I love Chesterton's comment in his book on Chaucer. A learned critic writing about Chaucer had said that 'it was possible that the poet had passed through a period of intense devotion towards the Virgin Mary'. Chesterton was amused. 'Yes, indeed,' he comments, 'it is indeed possible. It does occur from time to time. I don't understand though why Chaucer must have passed through this fit of devotion as if he had mariolatry like the measles. It doesn't usually visit its victim for a brief period. It is generally chronic and in some sad cases I have known quite incurable.' I love Mary, simply because she's God's mother. What's good enough for God should be good enough for us.

The second reason I love Mary is because of her purity. I love when the sun comes out just after a shower of rain. There's a freshness there, a purity in the air, a brightness about the light that you get at no other time. It's as if nature had confessed its sins, purified itself, entered into the state of grace, in a sacrament of reconciliation. I love that sunshine after rain because it reminds me of Mary. I love the springtime of the year, when the birds are peeping from the hedges and the leaves, testing their own texture, are a light delicate green, before the dust and darker green of summer. The 'glad green leaves', Thomas Hardy called them. I love the glad, green leaves. They remind me of Mary too. Mary is the sinless one I would like to be. She is the personification of that purity I know to be in the world, despite my own sins, despite the repeated atrocities of which human beings are capable. She is the Morning Star, Tower of Ivory, House of Gold. And I know that these things are not just rooted in my fancy; they are rooted in her Divine Motherhood, her Immaculate Conception, her fullness of Grace. 'Hail, full of grace ... Holy Mary, Mother of God.' Poets have rhapsodised about Mary. For Chaucer, she was 'glorious Virgin, of all flowers ... the flower'. But to my mind, the poet who best described her purity is our own Patrick Kavanagh. 'And I had a prayer like a white rose pinned on the Virgin Mary's blouse.' Can you imagine anything purer than that? A white rose on the Virgin Mary's blouse!

The third reason I love Mary is because of her concern. We may not like to admit it but we are all born with a prior interest in ourselves. We have to work very hard at developing an unselfish interest in others. We can be really concerned about the people around us, our family, our parish, our country, our world, or we can withdraw like the squirrel into the winter of our own life, with an endless

THESE MIGHT HELP TOO

supply of nuts. There are people who call themselves Christian who know nothing about their neighbours except their secrets. They know nothing about their wants and everything about their sins. They are inside-out Christians, upside-down Christians, with small hearts and bigger mouths. Mary was not like that. She was a model of community concern. She showed it in her devotion to her family, in her concern for other people, her prayerful encouragement of a crawling infant Church. When she climbed over hilly country to Elizabeth; when she precipitated the first miracle at Cana; when in her Magnificat she gave powerful expression to her passionate identification with the poor; when she took responsibility on Calvary for John and the whole Church, she was not settling for a comfortable winter, for a private devotional life. She was going public, really. She was exercising a motherly presence. She was accepting in full the implications of Christian love. For that concern, that softness towards others, I love Mary.

I love Mary because of her fidelity. Fidelity is a beautiful virtue. I think sometimes it's a feminine virtue ... a woman's virtue. The novelist Jane Austen certainly thought so. The theme of her novel *Persuasion* is that the love of woman is more constant than that of man. I think of people like St Monica and of all the Monicas the world over who have been unrelenting in their love for erring sons. And even as I say that, I think of God's faithfulness to the Jewish people and Christ's faithfulness to his Father's will, even to death on the cross. So I suppose you could argue the point. It's a matter of controversy. But no matter which side you take, there can be no controversy about the faithfulness of Mary. I think we've been inclined to misrepresent her. To conceive of her in our own minds and present her to the world as the anaemic woman, the insipid woman, the soup without stock. The obedient, pliant, passive instrument of God's will. 'Let what you have said be done to me ...' (Lk 1:38).

The woman who bowed her head to God's will, but who had no will of her own. The Milk of Magnesia woman with holy water in her veins rather than blood. It is of course a false image. It does justice neither to God's taste nor to Mary's character.[1] There stood by the cross of Jesus Mary his mother. She didn't faint, she didn't swoon, she didn't run (as the disciples did); she stood. And in her standing she was the faithful woman, the figure of fidelity. And when it was all over I venture to suggest that what the people around her were most conscious of was her incredible strength. For that strength in depth, for her ability to endure, for the purity and concern that we've talked about and most of all because she is Mother of God, I love the Virgin Mary.

Note

1.   See Joseph Cassidy, *These Might Help*, Veritas, 2000.

Jesus, Son of God

Eccles (Sir) 24:1-4, 8-12; Eph 1:3-6, 15-18; Jn 1:1-18

Twenty-seven years before the birth of Christ, a man called Herod the Great became King of most of Palestine. Because Palestine was part of the Roman Empire and because Herod ruled in connivance with Rome, he was unpopular with the Jewish patriots. Other factors contributed to his unpopularity – the fact that he was half-Greek, that sometimes he was half if not wholly mad and had people crucified and massacred when it suited his purpose. It was he who ordered the massacre of the Holy Innocents, for instance. Shortly before his death, he had two of his own sons strangled because he was suspicious of their political intentions. Even on his deathbed, he had his eldest son Antipater put to death on the grounds that he was plotting against him. Five days later, Herod died. I'd say there wasn't much of a wake in that family.

Herod's kingdom was divided among his sons – but Archelaus, who took possession of Judea, was such a bad ruler that the Romans eventually appointed a governor called Pontius Pilate, who would be remembered in history particularly for washing his hands. Meanwhile, the people of Palestine found it very difficult to make ends meet. Taxation was high, harvests were poor, starvation was either a constant threat or a debilitating reality. The number of beggars that we meet in the Gospel is very high for a largely agricultural community. The number of mentally unbalanced people is very high too, as is the number who were physically diseased. It wasn't a great time to be alive. Not in Palestine anyway!

What kept a lot of the Jewish people going was that God might intervene in the person of a Messiah. For the Jewish patriots, he was one who would smash the yoke of the

Roman oppressor. For religious people, he was someone 'who would come in Judgement, cleanse the world of evil, and by the power of God reign over a renewed and purified earth'.[1] Whatever their perception of the role he might play, both groups shared passionately the hope that he would come.

About the year AD 30, a small band of Jews, who seemed very honest and reliable, caused an almighty stir in Jerusalem by claiming that the Messiah had come. Now, they weren't the first to make such a claim. Others before them had made similar claims. However, no one before them had said what they were saying: that the Messiah who had come was Jesus of Nazareth; that he had been a preaching and healing sensation in Galilee and Judea; that as everybody knew he had been crucified on Calvary, but that, miracle of miracles, he had been raised from the dead. The Resurrection, they said, was the crowning proof that here was a personage even greater than Moses who was the fulfilment of all the prophecies and who had founded a community based on allegiance to himself which every repentant Israelite could join. It was sensational stuff that under the impetus of the Holy Spirit propelled them as missionaries in all directions – and that would cost most of them their lives.

One of these missionaries, John by name, is the author of today's Gospel (Jn 1-18). His primary reason for writing it was not merely to demonstrate that Jesus was the Messiah, or greater than Moses, or raised from the dead, however important these things are in themselves. There was something else about Jesus – essential to Jesus – that the Church believed and that he believed himself, which was more astonishing still. It's the pivotal truth, the ultimate truth, the most significant thing that anybody could ever say about Jesus of Nazareth. We need to look for a moment at today's prologue and at John's Gospel as a whole to see what it is.

THESE MIGHT HELP TOO

'In the beginning was the Word' [the *Logos*], John tells us, 'And the Word became flesh' (Jn 1:1, 14). The Word made flesh is Jesus. So what John is saying is that Jesus as the Word existed from the beginning. Whereas everything else in the world was created, the Word was not.[2] He just was. He just is. He is there eternally. John goes on to say then that the Word was with God. They existed together, in union with one another, sharing each other's life and love. The relationship of the Son to the Father is so close that John describes him, at the end of the prologue, as 'nearest to the Father's heart' (Jn 1:18). Then John makes what we might describe as the boldest statement of all. He says in a short but powerful sentence, 'And the Word was God' (Jn 1:1). Father and Son don't merely have unity in life; they have unity in divinity. They are two persons in one divine nature. So Jesus of Nazareth didn't just come on earth as God's emissary, or God's spokesman, or as the greatest of God's prophets. He came as God's Son. This is what got John sitting down, pen in hand in the first place to write his Gospel. This is what he was bursting to share with us all his missionary life. He tells us that himself, just before he put the pen down. 'These [things] are recorded,' he says, 'so that you may believe that Jesus is the Christ, the Son of God, and that believing this, you may have life through his name' (Jn 20:31). A believer like John had no option but to share this amazing truth with us. That Jesus is the Son of God is absolutely central to the Christian faith. The Christian faith revolves about it, is animated by it and stands or falls on the truth of it. May we always be in awe of it and rejoice in the wonder of it. May it give us (in all humility) an added sense of our own importance, and so deepen our faith in Jesus 'that we may have life through his name' (Jn 20:31).

Notes

1.   See William Neil, *Bible Commentary*, 1997, p. 351f.
2.   See Walter Kasper, *Jesus the Christ*, 1976, p. 170.

A Saviour for Everybody

Is 60:1-6; Ephes 3:2-3, 5-6; Mt 2:1-12

When I was growing up we had a turkey on only two days of the year: Christmas Day and the Epiphany – the first and last days of Christmas. Why was that? Well, we had one turkey for the Incarnation – the fact that the Word became flesh. But why had we the second turkey? What was it about the Epiphany that put it on a par with Christmas? Even in those days, wasn't it known in Ireland as *Nollag Beag* (Little Christmas)? The most it should have commanded then was a chicken. Nowadays, in the commercial world anyway, it barely commands attention, never mind a chicken! It has become almost completely detached, not just from Christmas itself but from the public consciousness. Is that such a bad thing? What is it about the Epiphany that should be retained and celebrated even as Christmas loses its profile and gets hidden behind the sales? Well – let's see!

One of the things we all need in life is friendship – whether we find it within the family or outside it. If we don't have it, it's very difficult to live without it. We need a friend for company – somebody to whom we can talk or with whom we can celebrate. Somebody with whom we can share the silence! It's when we are down or facing some huge trial in life that we need friendship most. To be able to pour your heart out into a sympathetic ear doesn't get rid of a problem but it certainly eases the pressure. It helps us to pick ourselves up and carry on for another while. Or if we have a funeral in the family, what we experience from the sympathisers is not pride in numbers (not primarily anyway) but consolation in friendship. People move in to fill the vacuum and minimise the loss. Even if there is no great crisis in our lives, it means a lot that a friend will keep in touch, just to see that we are alright. A phone call in a calm is better than a phone call in a storm because it is not occasioned by an event but by regard for you as a person. What matters most in a friend is constancy – once a friend, always a friend. Somebody said to me recently about a friend of her own that 'she has immediacy but no constancy'. You're no sooner gone than you're forgotten! I celebrated the funeral mass of a priest friend of mine a few years ago and after the funeral, another of his friends who had needed support in life said to me, 'He was the best foul weather friend a man could have'. Part of today's message is that Christ is our friend. The best foul-weather friend we could possibly have. If you are looking for constancy you'll find it in him. He keeps telling us that in the Gospel. 'I am the Good Shepherd' (Jn 10-14). 'Do not let your hearts be troubled ... Trust in God still – trust also in me ...' (Jn 14-1). 'Come to me all you who labour and are over-burdened and I will give you rest' (Mt 11-28). He's there for us, all the time, as our friend!

But the best of friends can only do so much. No more than ourselves, they are only contingent beings – they live only for a time and may be dead before us. The older we get, the more of our friends we lose. A life-long friendship remains a gift but it also becomes a memory. We are all vulnerable human beings doing our best to shore one another up but doomed ourselves to succumb to the forces that destroy our neighbours. The vulnerable can only support the vulnerable for so long. So what we all need – long term – is a friend who is also a Saviour. Somebody who is not vulnerable himself. Somebody who has defeated death. Somebody who will enable us to defeat death in our turn. Somebody who has opened the way to heaven.

Now that's what we get on the Feast of the Epiphany – not just a friend but a Saviour. That's what Christmas told us already: 'A Saviour has been born to you' (Lk 2:11).

That's what the Epiphany is telling us again. The readings are full of it. Isaiah has hints of it in the first reading. 'Above you the Lord now rises and above you his glory appears' (Is 60:2). The Gospel has even more of it. What the wise men wanted to know was, 'Where is the infant King of the Jews?' (Mt 2:2). The special emphasis in today's feast is that the Saviour King has come for everybody – not just for the Jewish people but for the Gentile nations as well, represented by the three wise men who have come from the East. So the embrace of the Saviour is from east to west. It excludes nobody. It takes in everybody. It encompasses the world. Despite the considerable claims of gold, frankincense and myrrh, the greatest gift in that crib today is the baby himself. Small wonder that we celebrate his presence and his promise with a second turkey. When in our native tradition we called the Epiphany *Nollag Beag*, we got the title wrong but the table right. The last day of Christmas is no less important than the first because, thanks to munificence from above, it is loaded with the promise of universal salvation. What a blessing it is, on this last day of Christmas, to have somebody in your life and mine who is both friend and Saviour!

The Life to Come

Is 40:1-5, 9-11; Titus 2:11-14, 3:4-7; Lk 3:15-16, 21-22
or Is 42:1-4, 6-7; Acts 10:34-38; Lk 3:15-16, 21-22

The biggest question you and I have to face is whether there is an afterlife or not. Most people hope there is, because the longest life here is so short, because our experience of life is so uneven, because so much good goes unrewarded and so much evil goes unpunished, because of the longing in the human heart for a life that is ongoing and complete, because of an instinctive human need for reunion with our loved ones, because we all know a few people who, because of an unforgiving disease or a crushing disability, deserved better than they got. Justice on its own is a powerful argument for another life. If a little girl, for instance, who is maimed by a terrorist bomb has no compensation in store in the life to come, then life itself is fundamentally disfigured and the universe in which we live is dominated by chance. We may make sense ourselves betimes, but the world around us, without a life to come, makes no ultimate sense at all.

The question of whether there's an afterlife depends on whether there's a God. An afterlife without a God would make no greater sense than this one. Is there a God? Sometimes the evening sky, all on its own, persuades me that there is. At other times, disproportionate human suffering suggests to me that there isn't. When an apparently random event occurs, like an earthquake killing thousands of people in one fell swoop, it does more than shake the earth, it shakes faith in providence as well. The thirteenth-century thinker and theologian Thomas Aquinas formulated five proofs for the existence of God which many people find utterly compelling. One of these focuses, not on the occasional disorder in nature, however brutal and inexplicable that may be, but on the prevailing beauty and design in the smaller world we inhabit ourselves and in the vastness of the universe. So much order bearing in on us is very hard to brush aside. Some of the world's most eminent scientists had no doubt at all about God's existence. Names that spring to mind are Isaac Newton, Charles Darwin and Albert Einstein. In a collection of interviews, published some twenty years ago now, with sixty prominent scientists, thirty-seven made no secret of the fact that they believed most emphatically in God. That kind of finding proves nothing in itself, except that high intelligence, scientific knowledge and belief in God co-exist comfortably together. Belief in God is not a superstitious survival of the unlettered mind. It is a common, compelling conviction in an enlightened age. In other words, if you do believe in God it doesn't mean that you're 'a thick'. It means you're in good company – with some of the brightest and the best.

Finally, did God himself give us any indication one way or the other as to whether he is there or not? Did he have a word with us about it at any stage along the way? He had a word with a small 'w' through the prophets. He had a word with a very big 'W' in the Word made flesh. The Word, the Second Person of the Blessed Trinity, was made flesh. For the past few weeks God has been reassuring us not just about his existence but about his persistent and overwhelming love. 'God loved the world so much that he gave his only Son so that everyone who believes in him may not be lost but may have eternal life' (Jn 3:16). What we celebrated on Christmas night and Christmas Day was the birth of God's Son and our Saviour. What was emphasised last Sunday, the feast of the Epiphany, is that this son of his is the saviour of the world. That's why the three wise men found their way to the crib. They came from the East – the world other than the Jewish world, the wider, outer world that Jesus was incorporating into his saving mission. What we are celebrating today in the Baptism of Jesus in the

Jordan is the blessing of heaven on that mission and more especially the descent of the Holy Spirit on Jesus himself. While he was 'at prayer, Heaven opened and the Holy Spirit descended on him in bodily shape, like a dove' (Lk 3:21, 22). We are being reminded that Jesus is the fulfilment of the prophecy we had from Isaiah in the first reading. 'Here is my servant whom I uphold, my chosen one in whom my soul delights; I have endowed him with my spirit that he may bring true justice to the nations' (Is 42:10). So the point I'm making is that God is in communication with us all the time. He'll be in touch with us again soon at the wedding feast of Cana when he changes the water into wine and gives colour to our watery faith. He'll be in touch with us throughout the year in the Gospels, in the people he heals, the stories he tells, the sermons he preaches to us. He'll give us the fullest message of all on Easter Sunday morning when he rolls away the stone and shows us the empty tomb. Today's feast, the Baptism of Our Lord, is only part of a pattern. God is there surely and he is speaking to us all the time. The Baptism of Our Lord is the beginning of a saving mission that will, with God's help and our own efforts, end for you and me when we join him up there in heaven. Or to put in another way: the river Jordan doesn't just flow into the sea, it flows into eternity as well. So it's the river we should travel on, as best we can!

Season
of
Lent

Preparing for Lent

If you were to ask people of my generation what we hated when we were young, one of the things was Castor Oil, because it represented everything with a horrible taste that was supposed to be good for us. We hated nettles – especially young nettles – because they gave them to us once a year to poison our taste buds and purify our blood. We hated girls too of course – the lads, I mean – but we got over that! And probably the thing we hated most of all was Lent. We hated Lent. No sweets, no meat as far as I remember, because every day was fast and abstinence, no let up until Easter Sunday when the blood flowed back into the year and it regained its normal character and complexion.

Nobody hates Lent now, because for a lot of people, Lent is nothing, and there is nothing in nothing to hate! If we felt there was a challenge there, I think one side of us would really hate it for the simple reason that challenges cost. Is Lent a challenge? Oh, I think it is, because of the uncertainty and brevity of our earthly existence. We hold on to life by the fingertips and sooner or later they give way. The Church reminds us of our contingent condition on Ash Wednesday: 'Remember man that you are dust and unto dust you shall return.' I was at three funerals between Wednesday evening and Friday morning. It's that way most weeks for you and for me. Most of my friends are on the mantelpiece in the parochial house in the form of mortuary cards. I cannot believe sometimes that so many of them are gone. We are reminded of death during Lent not to depress or dishearten us, but to encourage us to reflect on the transience of life. We are not going to be here forever. Now we either ignore that and keep on dancing until the trapdoor gives way, or we prepare for it as best we can. That doesn't mean we don't enjoy ourselves but it does mean we prepare to meet our God by clearing the false gods out of the way – the false gods of sin, selfishness, addiction and fantasy. Lent is about lining up your life and facing it in the right direction.

What should we do? I think we all need to be a bit more prayerful. I notice that during Lent there is always a bigger attendance at daily mass. That's great! We'll have our usual Lenten devotions in the evenings, as you know, and if we have a good attendance at those, great too! As well as that I think we would root Lent in its original soil if we were to reflect prayerfully on the scriptures. In most of our homes, I'm afraid, the Bible is a closed book. If we were to open it once a week during Lent, read one of the Gospel accounts of the Passion and pray about it, wouldn't we be taking the Calvary route to Easter? And mightn't it be a help with our own Calvaries as we journey through life? Then if we were all to say morning and night prayer, or say grace before and after meals as a family, or allocate a slot every day to pray with the children, confess our sins for Easter as we are obliged to do, then Lent mightn't be just a word but a transformation.

Secondly, we all need to be a bit more generous. God tells us through the prophet Isaiah, 'To share your bread with the hungry is the fast that pleases me' (Is 58:7-8). We get fed up of famine sometimes – hearing about it, I mean. But we are the lucky ones; we don't die from it. We need to keep reminding ourselves that hunger is always personal. Hunger always has a name and a face and eyes that should break our hearts. Don't let the hunger we see so often on TV blunt our sensibilities or deaden our conscience. If your mother or your child were dying of hunger you'd do anything to keep them alive. Let's keep them alive through Trócaire. Let's put them in the Trócaire box rather than the box for burial! May the Lord give us a generous heart. If your heart is in the right place, your hand will find its own way into your pocket.

Finally, we need to be a bit more honest. By that I mean facing up to reality – the real issues in our lives. We could ignore what we really need to do – like work, for instance – and do something else. That way, Lent becomes an exercise in evasion! Or if there is an obstacle in our lives between ourselves and God, or between ourselves and other people, then that's the most important thing to tackle and the most difficult to overcome because it will involve radical change. W. Somerset Maugham wrote a famous book called *Of Human Bondage*. It was about a young man's obsession with a girl. He was obsessed with her to the point of distraction. When it was over he said: 'She ran through me like a disease.' What he was conscious of now was liberation. He was a free man – for the first time in years. So let's work during Lent and let's pray for liberation from sin or addiction or the paralysis of indolence or indifference. The word 'Lent', as you know, means 'springtime'. May this Lent, above everything else, be a real springtime in our lives.

Jesus was Tempted Too

Deut 26:4-10; Rom 10:8-13; Lk 4:1-13

I was travelling by air to Fort Lauderdale. The first stage of the journey was from Shannon to Atlanta. That took about eight and a half hours, so when I sat in the plane for the second stage of the journey, I was very tired. People boarding a plane move very slowly, as you know. They have to explore the aisle in single file, searching, sometimes short-sightedly, for their seats, often finding other passengers, larger and more cumbersome than themselves, stolidly blocking their way. By the time they have found their seats, a place for their luggage in the racks overhead and squeezed themselves, with varying degrees of difficulty, into their allotted spaces, tired passengers like myself are on the verge of exhaustion. On this particular occasion I certainly was. I said to the man beside me, 'I hope we get started soon'. About forty minutes later I said exactly the same thing. We had been talking to one another all the time in between. 'But we have started,' he told me. 'We've been in the air for the past thirty minutes.' I couldn't believe it. I hadn't felt the plane taxi-ing into position, or racing down the runway. I hadn't felt its strained and sometimes shuddering trajectory as it propelled itself into the sky. A friend in America told me later that what I'd experienced or not experienced was a 'senior moment'. He was telling me – politely – that the lapse in awareness was one of the concomitants of old age. He was saying to me, 'You're losing it, pal!'

Could we all be losing it, in a different context? On a different journey? This is the first Sunday of Lent. What we are meant to do at this time of year is taxi into position on Ash Wednesday, race along the runway during the Lenten season in sustained preparation for the lift-off that is Easter. The trouble is that we could all arrive at Easter and be totally unaware of the Lent we've left behind. It couldn't happen to us at one time. The Lenten runway was far too bumpy for that. Now that Lent has been flattened out for us, so to speak, unless we are personally tuned into it, it won't be happening for us at all. We could find ourselves mid-Easter unawares!

That's less likely to happen to us if we take heed of today's Gospel. The point that is being made by Luke (and by Matthew and Mark as well) when they describe the temptations in the desert is that Jesus was fully human. Not semi-human, or 'kind of' human, but fully human. Just before they described the temptations, all three of them put the emphasis on Jesus as 'Son of God'. He was being baptised by John the Baptist in the Jordan and the voice came from heaven: 'This is my Son, the beloved. My favour rests on him' (Mt 3:17; Mk 1:11; Lk 3:22). Luke includes a genealogical table or a family tree that underlines the divine sonship as well. The conclusion we might draw, or that the early Christians might have drawn, is that if this was the Son of God, he must have had a charmed life as far as temptations were concerned. He wouldn't be put under the same kind of pressure as the rest of us. Instead of that, what we are witnessing today is huge pressure being put on Jesus by the evil one! What we are witnessing is a titanic struggle, a gigantic trial of strength, in which Satan tries to break down Christ's resolution to carry out his messianic mission and to give his life completely to God the Father. What's bothering Jesus is the hard road ahead. He is tempted to take the easy way as a wonder worker – turning stones into bread. He's tempted to be a political power rather than the suffering servant. He is tempted as Son of God to throw himself down from the parapet of the temple, force God to protect him from the fall and by implication from all the limitations of the human condition. He is tempted to live above his humanity, to live out of the flesh, so to speak. What Luke is emphasising is that while Jesus resisted these temptations, he didn't do so without a struggle. What he is saying in one sentence is that the Son of God, though sinless, was also the son of Adam. What's tempting for us was tempting for him.

We are the sons and daughters of Adam too. Life for all of us is a prolonged struggle between good and evil. Lent is a time when we intensify our efforts to resist the inroads of evil and to push out the frontiers of the good. It's a time to 'up the ante' on Satan, to gain an advantage over the enemy, to try to put the devil on the run. Is he winning the battle too easily at the moment? Is there evil in our lives of which we are anything but proud? Cleverly insinuated evil – and daunting and difficult to dislodge? If there is, let's take courage and heart from the victory of Christ and his example! Let's take particular note of his persistent prayerfulness during that desert experience and the strength he derived from that prayer. If prayer was necessary for him, it has to be necessary for us. If we allow ourselves 'to be led by the Spirit' as Jesus was in today's Gospel (Lk 4:1), we'll put in a good Lent. We'll be spared those 'senior moments'. And we won't arrive at Easter unawares.

THESE MIGHT HELP TOO

The Transfiguration

Gen 15:5-12, 17-18; Phil 3:17-4:1; Lk 9:28-36

I had a relative who left Ireland for America at the age of nineteen and who never came home for forty-two years. Not even for a visit! It was a long exile. When he sent word in 1968 that he was coming home to see us all, his sister dispatched me by car to pick him up at Shannon Airport. I had never seen him in my life but I knew that I'd recognise him because all our family were very handsome and distinguished. It's only in recent years that we're gone into a decline. When we arrived from the airport at his sister's house I stood at the kitchen door watching her as she greeted her long lost brother. I'll never forget the look of exaltation on her face. Her joy was so deeply felt, so clearly manifest, so luminously expressed that you could only describe it as Transfiguration.

When Jesus was on earth and people met him in the villages of Galilee, it never occurred to them that he was anything other than human. They must have been impressed by his preaching and his healing and his charismatic personality, but all they saw before them was a man. We probably see him as Son of God first and human after that, whereas they saw him as human only. The fact that he was a healer or a miracle worker would not have persuaded them that he was God. It would have persuaded them that he was a man of God, like the earlier prophets, but they'd never have concluded that he was God's only son. The men who were close to him must have sensed something very special in him but they couldn't have been sure of what it was. Then one day, at a place called Caesarea Philippi, Jesus put to them a straight question. 'Who do people say the Son of Man is?' (Mt 16:13). They said, 'Some say he is John the Baptist, some Elijah, and others Jeremiah or one of the other prophets' (Mt 16:14). 'But you, who do you say I am?' (Mt 16:15). It was Peter who spoke up. 'You are the Christ, the Son of the Living God' (Mt 16:16). Now, according to Matthew's Gospel, he was the first one ever to say that. It was an outstanding act of perception and faith. It was more than that. It was a view of things that was inspired from above. Jesus was quick to acknowledge that. 'Simon, son of Jonah,' he said, 'you are a happy man. Because it was not flesh and blood that revealed this to you, but my Father in Heaven' (Mt 16:17). He was saying that with a bit of help from on high, Peter had got it right.

Then, six days later, to show them that he had got it right, he took Peter, James and John up the mountain to see the Transfiguration – to see the dazzling presence of the divine in him. In the case of the relative I spoke about, transfiguration was an explosion of inner joy. In his case it's the explosion of hidden divinity. A man is the Son of God and the truth of it is manifested in beauty.

Now Peter, James and John and the rest of the apostles were in for a rough time. Since this Jesus was the Messiah, they expected him to take Jerusalem by storm. Instead of that, they witnessed the scourging at the pillar, the crowning with thorns, the carrying of the cross, the Crucifixion. Was their faith being tested? You bet it was being tested. Did they remember the Transfiguration? Hopefully they did. They were meant to remember it, to carry them through, to keep up their morale until the Risen Christ would appear again in their midst.

Has your faith been tested in the course of your life? Mine certainly has. And it has been tested most of all by the randomness and unevenness of human suffering. I find it very difficult to understand why some people suffer as much as they do – only some people – and why some of the people I loved suffered as much as they did. Jesus promised us that everything would be evened out in heaven, that God's Providence stretches over both time and eternity. The disciples had the Transfiguration to help them through one rough patch. We have the Transfiguration and the Resurrection to help us through our rough patches here on earth. To help us dazzle our doubt! We need to hold on to them. To remember them. To remind ourselves of them. To be encouraged by them. To see the light in them. To see 'the hole in Heaven's gable'. I suppose there are two ways of looking at our human condition. Either we are stumbling around in a darkness that will never be dispelled at all, or we are being led by Jesus through the darkness, to the Father. The Transfiguration and Resurrection would suggest that the second scenario is true. Jesus leading the way gives meaning and a destination to our journey. After all, it isn't everyone who can light up a mountain and leave us an empty tomb!

One More Year

Ex 3:1-8, 13-15; 1 Cor 10:1-6, 10-12; Lk 13:1-9

What did you make of God in the first reading? What impression of him did you get? An angry God? An uncaring God? A compassionate God? Before we come to a conclusion about that, could we recall a few of the details? God manifested himself or made himself intensely present to Moses on Mount Horeb. The burning bush is a dramatic symbol of that manifestation. He told him that he was his people's God, the God of Abraham and Isaac and Jacob. The naming of them suggests that each of them was not just known to him personally but beloved of him as well. He even told Moses his own name – 'I am who I am' – even though its meaning would be beyond his comprehension. Most significantly, in terms of God's attitude, he told Moses that he had chosen him to lead his people out of slavery in Egypt. What he said leaves no doubt whatsoever about the kind of God he is. 'I have seen the miserable state of my people in Egypt. I have heard their appeal to be free of their slave drivers. Yes, I am well aware of their sufferings. I mean to deliver them out of the hands of the Egyptians ... and bring them to a land rich and broad ... where milk and honey flow' (Ex 3:7-8). An angry God? An uncaring God? A compassionate God? I think he speaks for himself.

It is because our God is compassionate and because he wants to deliver us, not just from slavery in Egypt but from the slavery of sin and death, that he calls on us in the Gospel, through his son Jesus Christ, to repentance. In fact, in what is a very short extract, he uses the word 'repent' twice. 'Unless you repent you will all perish' (Lk 13:3, 5). And lest we be in any doubt as to the importance of repentance, he calls for it a third time, in the parable of the barren fig tree.

THESE MIGHT HELP TOO

I'm no expert on horticulture, but it seems that when a fig tree was planted in Our Lord's time in Palastine it was given three years of growth before the fruit was picked. After that it was expected to deliver. This fig tree in the parable grew for six years and delivered nothing. It didn't give a fig, so to speak. It sat there, nestling into the ground, pushing its roots deeper and deeper into the nutrients of its neighbours and hadn't a thing to show for it except a flourish of leaves. The owner of the vineyard – a reasonable and practical man – saw no solution for this impostor other than to cut it down. After all, it was burgling the soil around it only to replenish itself. The man who looked after the tree, the vinedresser – who had a special care for every rooted thing – said, 'please, please, give it another chance; I'll do my best with it. If it doesn't produce fruit in one more year, you can cut it down' (Lk 13:9).

The owner of the vineyard stands for God. The barren fig tree stands for the people. The message we are getting is that the people from whom God expected fruit are as barren as the fig tree. A flourish of leaves perhaps – a tentative fluttering – but nothing of substance. No fruit! No justice! No acknowledgement of God! No observance of his commandments! No virtue! Leaves only – and leave taking! If people are spiritually and morally sterile, they must be cut down. If judgement is passed on them now, then judgement is passed in justice. But God's nature goes beyond justice into patience, and understanding and compassion. 'Yes, yes,' he says to the vinedresser (whom some think stands for Jesus), 'I won't condemn, I won't give up on them. I'll give them another year. Since time may bring a turning, I'll give them time.'

I'd be slow to compare anyone in this congregation to the barren fig tree. I'm sure that figs of all kinds have flourished in your life – in the way you have done your work, looked after your families, said your prayers, kept the commandments, consulted your conscience, acknowledged your weaknesses, confessed your sins. At the same time, there can be an uneven distribution of fruit on any fig tree – barren branches in lives that God would wish us to make fruitful. Maybe there is pruning to be done in your life and mine – the pruning of an enmity, a selfishness, a peevishness perhaps, that makes life impossible for those with whom we live. Maybe we need to dig a little bit, as the vinedresser proposed to do. Whatever we need to do to make our lives more fruitful, we need to do quickly. We need to do now! There is an urgency, as well as compassion, at the heart of today's parable. When you think about it, all that was given to the fig tree was one more year!

The Prodigal Son

Josh 5:9-12; 2 Cor 5:17-21; Lk 15:1-3, 11-32

Some time ago, when I was going on a visit to the States, I
brought some dollars with me. I'm not going to tell you how
much I brought. All I'll say is that I expected to have less
coming back than I had going out. What I didn't expect was
to have none at all. The day after I arrived in America I lost
all my dollars. I searched the obvious places – pockets,
suitcase, wardrobe. They were nowhere to be found. I must
have pulled them out of my trousers pocket with my
handkerchief or else somebody did it for me with finger and
thumb. Either way, I was on my uppers. It was a case of
'Brother, can you spare a dime?' I slept uneasily that night.
The following morning I started searching again. Eventually,
I found them in the place where I had put them for safe
keeping. Another senior moment! I was very relieved to have
found them. More than that – I was delighted! You could
even say that I was overjoyed. I didn't kill a fatted calf like
the father in today's Gospel. I didn't throw a party as he did.
But I did have a little private party all to myself.

Why am I telling you this? Well, because it's true, and
because we hate to lose things, whether it's money, or a
ring, or the key of the car or the key of the house. And we
love finding them! God is the same, except what he hates
is losing people. Losing them to their own sin and
selfishness, losing any one of us for whom Jesus died on
the cross. And God loves finding us again. Loves when we
come back to him. His delight in this regard is largely
dependent on our repentance. That point is beautifully
recorded by St Luke in chapter fifteen of his Gospel. If you
are not familiar with that chapter, could we take a look at
it now?

There are three stories or parables in Luke 15. Jesus tells them as a response to a complaint. The complaint made by the Scribes and the Pharisees is that he was too friendly with sinners. The first story is about the man with a hundred sheep who leaves the ninety-nine and goes after the one who was lost! The second story is about the woman with the ten coins who loses one and who does not stop searching until she finds it. The third – today's story – is about the father who saw his son go away and who never had a day's peace until he came back. So, the story of the Prodigal Son is part of a trilogy and the three stories are about restlessness – a restless God who is in continual pursuit of the sinner; 'The Hound of Heaven' that Francis Thompson talked about in his poem of the same name. The stories are about celebration too – the upsurge of joy in heaven when the lost one is finally found. 'There will be more rejoicing in heaven over one repentant sinner than over ninety-nine virtuous men who have no need of repentance' (Lk 15:7). More than anything else of course, the three stories are about the fullness of God's forgiveness. As soon as the son appears on the horizon, forgiveness runs out to meet him – envelopes him, embraces him, absolves him without a hint of reproach. The brother's forgiveness runs nowhere. It won't even go in to the party. It digs in its heels and ends up in protest! There's a startling contrast in the story between the forgiveness that comes from above and the forgiveness that comes from the side; between God's forgiveness and our own. We think about what the sinner should get – measured, appropriate. God thinks of what he should be given – generously, extravagantly. Finding is fundamental. Coming to life is everything. 'Because your brother here was dead and has come to life; he was lost and is found' (Lk 15:32).

There is one other thing that the parables are all about – especially today's one – and that is the importance of repentance. Paul emphasises it as well in the second reading when he says, 'Be reconciled to God' (2 Cor 5:20). While I was on the visit to the States that I already mentioned, I went to see the film 'The Passion of the Christ', directed by Mel Gibson. You may not have seen it but it was causing a great deal of controversy at the time. Some people thought it might have been shaded better, that it was lacking in subtlety, that a less violent presentation would have been more effective. Whether you thought that or not, it was a horrendous portrayal of the suffering of Jesus from the Agony in the Garden to the Crucifixion. I couldn't look at some of it. The scourging was so relentless that the Crucifixion itself was a relief. We don't think enough about the Passion nowadays. Even the crucifixes we have are sanitised – sanitised representations of his death rather than realistic reminders of his suffering. They tore him to shreds in the scourging. We all added to that by our sins and we still do. His body was one trembling mass of gore and gouged flesh. I said to a fellow priest, 'Why did he have to suffer so much?' 'Hard to understand,' he said. 'Sin must be a horrible thing in the sight of God.' Unless we're aware of that, unless we see sin as horrible too, we won't be moved to repentance. A Saviour who suffered so much, a God as forgiving as he is, deserves a better response! May we make that response during this Lenten season. May we make the Ash Wednesday exhortation our own. May we turn away from sin and be faithful to the Gospel.

The Woman in Adultery

Is 43:16-21; Phil 3:8-14; Jn 8:1-11

I know this is very unfair now, but do you remember what the Gospel was about last Sunday week? No? It was about the barren fig tree. The tree that stood for six long years without giving a fig. Did the owner of the vineyard cut it down? No – he gave it one more year. In the same way, God in his mercy gives sinners like us another opportunity to repent. Do you remember what last Sunday's Gospel was about? I think you do! It was the story of the Prodigal Son. God's forgiveness was at its most abundant yet again. Justice might have given the repentant son bed and board for a while. It took mercy to kill the calf. Today we have the story of the woman in adultery. For the third time – in three Sundays – divine mercy has been at full tide. The last few weeks of Lent have been nothing if not mercy-full!

Apart from what we learn in today's Gospel, we know little or nothing about the woman in adultery. We know that she must have been married, because in Jewish law what constituted adultery was sexual intercourse between a married woman and a man other than her husband.[1] Whereas, in the culture of the time, she would be faulted for cheating on her husband, he would not be faulted for cheating on her. It was an unequal situation – an unfair situation. Did she resent that? Was her adultery, apart from being a pursuit of pleasure, a form of protest as well? We don't know. Was it simpler than that? Had she sinned with a man whom she had loved all her life and whom she would have certainly married had she been given the choice? Was the marriage in which she found herself now a very unhappy one? Did she feel that she was trapped? Was she hostage to a husband who was indifferent, abusive or himself unfaithful? We don't know. Was she a frivolous kind of girl, who made a reckless intrusion into a happy marriage, and who indulged herself heedlessly at another woman's expense? Did she realise the seriousness of what she was doing – that in committing the sin of impurity, she was sinning against justice as well? Was she a hardened sinner, a predator on the loose – whose only consideration was her own pleasure? Or was she a likeable and loveable woman, whose primary weakness was a lustfulness that she had striven all her life to keep in check? What were the circumstances in which this woman sinned? What were the forces at work in her life? We just don't know.

The Pharisees didn't need to know! Even if they knew her well and understood some of the circumstances, what mattered to them was that they had a sinner in their sights. If they didn't bring the stones with them – and the Gospel doesn't say that they did – they wouldn't have far to go to find them. The beauty of the situation from their point of view was that they might kill two birds with the one stone. The woman would be dead and Jesus would be discredited. That was the plan! 'Master,' they said, 'this woman was caught in the very act of committing adultery and Moses has ordered us in the Law to condemn women like this to death by stoning – what have you to say?' (Jn 8:4, 5). What was Jesus to do? If he gave it as his opinion that she be put to death, his reputation for compassion would die with her. If he urged that she be spared, he'd be in conflict with the Law of Moses. It was the classic dilemma. And the Pharisees were closing in.

One thing is clear from Our Lord's response. He had no time, in this situation, for the Pharisees. He had no time, whatsoever, for their rush to judgement! He understood better than they did the complexity of the human condition and the weaknesses in all of us that might precipitate us, against our better instincts, into sin. He understood as well that there was more to this woman than her adultery. There was a history there. A record of struggle and achievement. No human being is one thing alone. He had warned the people many times against simplistic judgements. To a legalistic group who interpreted a sabbath healing of his in terms of sabbath violation alone, he said, 'Do not keep judging according to appearances; let your judgement be according to what is right' (Jn 7:23). He condemned external judgement in much stronger terms in Matthew's Gospel. 'Judge not and you will not be judged. Why do you observe the splinter in your brother's eye and never notice the plank in your own? Hypocrite! Take a plank out of your own eye first and then you will see clearly enough to take the splinter out of your brother's eye' (Mt 7:3, 5). Every accuser gathered around him now had a plank in his eye and maybe a skeleton in his cupboard. It didn't stop any of them from pointing the finger. It didn't stop Jesus from using his own finger to write on the ground. Why did he do this? Was he just idling away the time? No, he wasn't. He was digging a hole for the Pharisees! He would bury them with only one sentence: 'If there is one of you who has not sinned, let him be the first to throw a stone at her' (Jn 8:7). It was a burial without stones!

The final scene between Jesus and the woman is truly beautiful, in the serenity that surrounds it, the gentleness with which he treats her, the dignity that he restores to her. Not that he condoned her sin. He didn't. He urged her not to repeat it. 'Go away now and sin no more' (Jn 8:11). I think she must have known, as she went away, that here was one person on earth who truly loved her. When each of us knows that we are loved in that way too, why is it that we don't make a better effort to repent?

Note

1.   Wilfrid Harrington OP, *Mark, New Testament Message*, Veritas, p. 155.

THESE MIGHT HELP TOO

Entry into Jerusalem

Luke 19:28-40

Apart from the palm itself, with what do you associate Palm Sunday? I'd say it might be the long Gospel! We used to stand for that in the old days, and in many places people still do. The endurance on our part is meant to be in solidarity with what Jesus endured, especially on Good Friday. We are often not too far into the Passion story, however, before we begin to wonder how much longer it's going to take. We like our short cuts in this country. All the trodden paths that cut corners bear witness to that. Despite our impatience with long liturgies, we pause on our way out of mass to select a sprig of palm to take home with us. There is a special satisfaction in that, not just because we are getting something at the church door – for a change – but because in a very personal way we are drawing Jesus that bit closer to ourselves and recognising him as our King. We'll enthrone him quietly when we get home by placing the palm behind his picture or else above his cross. The palm will fade and wither as another year goes by. When we find its green replacement the following year we'll renew our allegiance again.

We are right about the King idea! Very much so! The first thing that strikes me about the approach of Jesus to Jerusalem, as described today in Luke's Gospel (Lk19:28-40), is that this is no ragged arrival of an obscure provincial prophet, but the triumphant entry into his capital city of a long awaited Saviour-King. Because he is riding on an ass he comes in peace. But because he's riding on an ass, he comes in purple too. The royal and messianic overtones so evident in Luke's description have their origins in the first and second book of Kings and in the prophet Zechariah. In

Kings, Book One, King Solomon is mounted on a mule as he is led to his royal anointing (1 Kings 1:38). What the prophet Zechariah foretold about the coming Messiah-King is fully and precisely reflected in Luke's depiction of Jesus: 'See now your King comes to you; he is victorious, he is triumphant, humble and riding on a donkey, on a colt, the foal of a donkey (Zech 9:9).

Even the garments they threw on the road were the people's tribute to royalty. The same thing occured in the Old Testament to a man called Jehu when he became King of Israel. 'Whereupon, they took all their cloaks and spread them under him on the bare steps; they sounded the trumpet and shouted, "Jehu is King"' (2 Kings 9:13). Even the detail that the donkey was a colt on which nobody had sat as yet has a royal implication that is unique to Jesus. The old Israel is dying as the procession proceeds. Jesus will preside over a kingdom that is completely new.

The second thing that strikes me about the entry into Jerusalem is that it is one of the happiest episodes in the entire Gospel. All the disciples are in jubilant mood. They are praising God 'at the top of their voices' and 'calling down blessings on the King who comes' (Lk 19:38). As well as celebrating the 'now' they are looking forward to the future and remembering the past. They are looking forward to the kingdom of which Jerusalem will be the capital and they are remembering the stories he told, the miracles he performed and the people he made whole along the way. Today is a multiple day. An irrepressible day. The palms in the air have a life of their own. They dance in concurrence without assistance from anybody. The disciples are so exuberant, so wildly and deliriously happy, that the Pharisees, with characteristic severity, urge Jesus to restrain them. However, today is not the Pharisees' day! Their day will come, unfortunately. Today their protests are in vain. If an attempt were made to subdue or silence the disciples, the very 'stones themselves would cry out' (Lk 19:40).

THESE MIGHT HELP TOO

The third thing that strikes me about his entry into Jerusalem is that it must have been one of the loneliest occasions in Jesus' life. Even though some of the Gospel references to his death are post-Easter interpretations, as Jesus approached the city he must have been filled with fear for his own safety. If his enemies could kill him, they would. From the beginning of his mission he had been on a collision course with the Pharisees. Time and time again they fought with him for breaking the sabbath (Mk 2:24). When he cured the blind and dumb demoniac, they accused him of being in league with the devil (Mt 12:24). When he forgave the paralytic his sins, the Scribes berated him for blasphemy (Mk 2:7). If John the Baptist had been executed by Herod it was unlikely that Jesus would be spared. When, on one occasion, the Pharisees warned him that the same Herod was indeed planning to kill him, Jesus was only too well aware that the danger was real. It was a danger from which he wouldn't shrink. 'You may go and give that fox this message. Learn that today and tomorrow I cast out devils and on the third day attain my end. But for today and tomorrow and the next day I must go on, for it would not be right for a prophet to die outside Jerusalem' (Lk 13:31-33).

'Jesus saw his own fate prefigured in that of the prophets.'[1] Just as they had to face their destiny in Jerusalem, so would he. Had he not said himself, 'The Son of Man will be delivered into the hands of men.' (Mk 9:31)? Beneath the cheers and the hosannas on his triumphal journey Jesus had to be full of foreboding. Those of us who know now how much he suffered for our sake must this week be filled with gratitude. Let us enter fully and prayerfully into his Passion during the coming grace-filled days.

Note

1.   Walter Kasper, *Jesus the Christ*, Paulist Press, 1976, p. 117.

Easter

Triduum

The Passover Lamb

Ex 12:1-8, 11-14; 1 Cor 11:23-26; Jn 13:1-15

Do you know how many people there would have been in Our Lord's time in the city of Jerusalem for the feast of the Passover? A hundred to a hundred and fifty thousand! The city population itself was about thirty thousand, and at least one hundred thousand more would arrive from all parts of Palestine before the Passover and during the festival itself. Roads were choked with pilgrims, Jerusalem packed to overflowing. Most of the pilgrims hadn't a hope of getting lodgings of course so they'd have to find a space for a tent. The highlight of the festival was a Passover meal consisting of lamb, unleavened bread and bitter herbs. Because the place was so crowded, the lambs would be slaughtered in the temple area and the meals would take place in the houses or tents. Those who had neither house nor tent would have to eat their meal in a courtyard or alleyway or on the roof of a house. Since the celebration took place after sunset and went on far into the night, 'eating out' wasn't as comfortable then as it is now. The main reason for that was because in springtime, when the festival took place, the nights were very cold. There is a reference to the coldness of the night in Mark's Gospel, when Peter, before his denials of Jesus, was warming himself at the fire (Mk 14:54).[1] One of the problems the indoor diners had, as the night wore on, was keeping the children awake for Bible instruction – a problem we have at Mass ourselves, on occasions, with children and adults alike! Not your fault!

Why did the Jewish people make so much of the Passover? The word itself has an ancient ring to it – a muffled, inaccessible quality. It's like an old coin in a new currency. 'Flyover' makes immediate sense. 'Passover' goes over our heads. What exactly is it all about? Well, in the old days when the Jewish people were nomadic shepherds they had a spring feast that, among other things, had to do with lambs. When the lambs were born, they'd offer one of them to God in sacrifice, because everything belonged to him and he above all was entitled to the first fruits. When they had killed the lamb and offered their sacrifice, they'd smear its blood at the entrance to their house or tent to show that they had recognised their God. All that is described in greater detail in tonight's first reading (Ex 12:1-8, 11-14).

Now, early in the thirteenth century BC, while the Jews, as slaves in Egypt, were celebrating their feast, a plague broke out among the Egyptians. They suffered heavily. The Jewish people did not. The plague 'passed over' them. The blood had saved them. That's how they understood it. God was looking after his own! The Passover took on deeper levels of meaning when God brought them first through the Red Sea, then through the desert, then through the Ten Commandments which formed the core of a covenant by which he would be their God and they would be his people. So the Passover from slavery in Egypt to freedom in God was of immense importance to the Israelites. It was important historically because it made a united people out of a scattering of slaves. It was important theologically because it indicated God's desire to draw all people to one another and to himself. No wonder some of the pilgrims to Jerusalem were prepared to celebrate the Passover on the roofs of the houses. Some things need to be proclaimed from the housetops, including, of course, what God had done for them in the past and would surely do in the future!

On the night of the Last Supper, in one of the thousands of supper rooms in the city of Jerusalem, what God would do for his people in the future was already taking shape in the person of Jesus Christ. Paul tells us about it in tonight's second reading (1 Cor 11:23-26). John gives us his account in tonight's Gospel. 'The Lord Jesus took some bread,' Paul

THESE MIGHT HELP TOO

says. 'This is my body which is for you. This cup is the new covenant in my blood' (1 Cor 11:24, 25). What Jesus is telling us is that his body and blood are being offered up for our sake. John gives us the same message in the Gospel. 'Jesus knew,' he tells us, 'that the hour had come for him to pass from this world to the Father' (Jn 13:1). What we are being told, in its essence, is that Jesus is the Passover Lamb. He is offering himself up in voluntary self-sacrifice for the salvation of the world. The plague of sin and death will pass over our heads. His blood on the cross will be our salvation. We will be delivered from a slavery far worse than that of Egypt. We will be fed with the Eucharist on our desert journey through life. We will be expected to wash each other's feet in the course of that journey. If we are faithful to the new covenant Christ has sealed with his blood, we can hope, with some confidence, to make it to the Promised Land. Some things indeed ought to be proclaimed from the housetops. What we proclaim and give thanks for on this Passover evening is the salvation won for us by the Passover Lamb!

Note

1. See Joachim Jeremias, *The Eucharistic Words of Jesus*, Fortress Press, 1977.

The Sign of the Cross

Is 52:13-53:12; Heb 4:14-16, 5:7-9; Jn 18:1-19:42

I wonder would you have any idea when you first came in contact with the cross? You wouldn't remember of course, but your mother probably made the sign of the cross on your forehead soon after you were born. Your parents, your godparents, would have made the sign on your forehead at baptism. The priest would have anointed you again on the forehead with the oil of chrism – christened you for your mission in life. Even while you were still in the womb, there would have been physical contact of which you were totally unaware, because your mother would have blessed herself many times in her prayer for a safe delivery. You would have been in touch with the cross at one remove. We were all expected and born and baptised and christened under the sign of the cross.

Do you remember the first time you saw a cross – became conscious of the cross? It was probably in your home or perhaps in the church. You may have noticed it at the end of a rosary beads or hanging on a wall. It's hard to know. I think I noticed it for the first time on the mantelpiece in my parents' room. I certainly knew as a very young child that it was there. I noticed it in the church because it wasn't up at the altar at all, it was on the side wall, and that was unusual. There are at least thirty-four crosses in this church and perhaps more! The cross is all about us.

Do you remember the first heavy cross you got in your own life? The first really heavy cross? The one that came close to breaking your heart? Or succeeded in doing so – for a time anyway? Was it a help to you that this was God's will perhaps or that you were carrying your cross with Christ? It wasn't a help to me at the beginning anyway. I was too upset at first and then too angry with God, especially that he would allow the people I loved most to suffer so much. Because the heaviest crosses can be indirect crosses. Not the one you are carrying, but the one somebody else is carrying while you have to stand helplessly by. Another very heavy cross is the cross of your own making because it's weighted down as well with regret and remorse and 'if only'. Many of us know from sad experience that the hardest cross you have to carry is the cross you make for yourself.

I've learned, as I'm sure you have, that anger or bitterness or self-pity don't make crosses any lighter. I'm a bit better now at offering up whatever cross I have with Christ, because that's a more positive approach; it helps to make sense of it and it's what he wants me to do. 'If anyone wants to be a follower of mine, let him renounce himself and take up his cross every day and follow me. For anyone who wants to save his life will lose it; but anyone who loses his life for my sake, that man will save it' (Lk 9:23-24). Carrying a cross can be productive or redemptive. It can have huge leverage. It can be a sacrificial prayer for others and for oneself.

I have learned too as I go through life that I need Christ's love and that I'm lucky to have it. He proved his love for me on the cross and that love cost him dearly. Today is the day in the year which brings that home to us more than any other. Isaiah puts it into words for us in the first reading: 'Ours were the sufferings he bore, ours the sorrows he carried … He was pierced through for our faults, crushed for our sins' (Is 53:4-5). St John has just reminded us in the Gospel of how Jesus was hemmed in by the hatred of some, the vacillation of one, the sinfulness of all. What's remarkable about him is his willingness to endure. The sacrificial spirit in which he bore his suffering is best exemplified perhaps by his tenderness from the cross towards his mother and St John. 'Woman this is your son … This is your mother' (Jn 19:26). As beneficiaries of his love and concern, they stand for all of us. They weren't the only recipients of his love. All of us gathered here and billions we don't know at all were standing there too. His love is universal. And when we talk about his love being universal, we are not just talking about Jesus in his humanity. We are talking about him in his divinity too. The God in him suffered on the cross as well. And the fact that God exposed himself freely to that suffering and experienced it for our sake is at once the most startling and reassuring expression of solidarity that we could ever imagine. One with us in the flesh, one with us in the pain!

So the cross is a wonderful sign of God's love. From our conception until now, all of us have grown up in its love-laden shadow. May the Good Friday we celebrate never become a single day – an isolated day – in our liturgical year. May it retain its status and exert its influence. May the cross of Christ be a symbol of hope and meaning and love and victory, not just for today, but all through our lives. May the Lord help you and all of us with the cross we are carrying now, because with his help and our own courage and the bit of fight that we can muster and that we need to muster, we shall overcome!

V for Victory

Rom 6:8-11; Lk 24:1-12

It's not generally appreciated I think, but tonight is the climax of the Christian year. In the early Church it was unthinkable that a Christian wouldn't attend the Easter Vigil. As a matter of fact, the test for the Christian was whether he or she attended the vigil or not. If you stayed away you couldn't really believe, they felt, that Christ was risen. One of the early fathers, a man called Tertullian, was very worried about a marriage between a Christian and a pagan, in case the pagan wouldn't allow the Christian to go to the Easter Vigil. St Augustine, who was himself baptised during an Easter Vigil by St Ambrose on 25 April 387, described Holy Saturday night as 'the mother of all vigils'. It's the highpoint of the Christian year because it's a big victory celebration. V is not just for Vigil; it's for victory as well, Christ's victory over the discouraging darkness of sin and the bewildering darkness of death.

What we are celebrating tonight is quite extraordinary. In our experience, Death makes no concessions whatsoever to life. Our cemeteries are full of monuments to its unrelenting dominance. So what's all this talk about resurrection? Maybe one possible explanation is that Jesus was not dead at all? Well, the trouble with that of course is that the New Testament accounts insist very emphatically that he was. We are told that he was crucified between two thieves (Mk 15:27); that he said, 'It is accomplished', and gave up his spirit (Jn 19:30). We are told that there was no need to break his legs, because he was already dead and that when they pierced his side with a lance 'out flowed blood and water' (Jn 19:3-34). We are told that Pilate would not agree to hand over the body to Joseph of Arimathaea until he had been assured by the centurion that Christ was really dead (Mk 15:45). In addition to all that, we have the details about the body being wrapped in a shroud and laid in a tomb (Lk 23-31) that was sealed with a stone (Mk 15:46). To cap it all, if you like, we are assured that Mary of Magdala and Mary the mother of Joset were watching all this as it happened and taking very careful note of where Jesus was laid (Mt 15:49).

Accepting the fact that Jesus was dead, maybe his resurrection happened only because his followers expected it to happen? Perhaps because they wanted it to happen, they persuaded themselves that it had? The trouble with this theory is that the disciples didn't expect Jesus to rise at all. In terms of expectation, they had been crucified with him. They were a scattered remnant now – shattered and demoralised. Their immediate concern had to be with their own survival. The women in tonight's Gospel didn't go to the tomb expecting the resurrection. They went 'with the spices they had prepared' in order to anoint the body (Lk 24:1). Finding the tomb empty and filling with a resurrection at this stage, they rushed to tell the apostles, only to be accused of talking 'nonsense' (Lk 24:11). When Peter, running to the tomb himself, found some evidence of a resurrection in the absence of Christ's body and the binding cloths that were lying there, his reaction was one of 'amazement' (Lk 24:12). That was the general reaction among the disciples. They were absolutely astonished by the resurrection, as well they might. Death in their experience, as in ours, didn't give in that easily. Mountains had been moved. The laws of nature had been reversed. Death had succumbed to its own demise and had immortalised an Easter morning. The disciples couldn't be other than astonished. Astonishment was an appropriate response. In our reaction to the resurrection we need to be astonished too. Everything has been changed by it and changed by it irrevocably. 'Death has no power over him anymore' (Rom 6:9). That's the way St Paul put it in

THESE MIGHT HELP TOO

tonight's reading. The Death that seems to us to be so dominant and conclusive is not really that dominant and conclusive at all. Ultimately it has been put in its place. It has been routed in a garden. It is sulking behind a stone.

However, it still retains its power in this life and all of us have died a little since this time last year. There isn't one of us that hasn't experienced disappointment or discouragement during the past year and these things are a form of dying as well. Despite the good we have done, there isn't one of us who hasn't sinned, and sin is a particularly bitter form of death because it reminds us of our own frailty and it weakens our friendship with Christ. So tonight – as on every other night – we are all a bit broken. No matter how confident or cheerful we may seem there's a need for healing, for consolation within. We need to feel forgiven, that we're worthwhile, that life has meaning, that in the final analysis we are not obliterated by death and destined for oblivion. It is Christ who heals us, Christ who loves us, Christ who forgives us, Christ who redeems us, Christ who conquers for us and lets us share in his victory. 'If in union with Christ, we have imitated his death, we shall also imitate him in his Resurrection' (Rom 6:5). So we rejoice tonight as believing Christians in the resurrection of our Saviour. Let me give you, as I do every year, the Easter greeting: 'Christ is Risen'; 'He is Risen indeed, Alleluia.'

Season
of
Easter

Resurrection

Acts 10:34, 37-43; Col 3:1-4; Jn 20:1-9

I have noticed, in the course of my life, that the death of somebody we love is doubly lethal in that it has an immediate impact and a continuing existence. In a sense, it never goes away. When somebody to whom we are deeply attached draws a final breath, our grief is overwhelming. Death never confines itself to a single target. It does collateral damage as well. It breaks the hearts of those who stand helplessly by. Apart from its immediate impact, death has a continuing existence in that as well as taking the person away from us for good it leaves an emotional residue in its wake. This is especially true if the person we love dies before his or her time, or in prolonged agony. The effect of that is to fuel or intensify our grief. People accept the fact of death of course and get on with their lives as best they can, but a love that is deep and close does not die with its object. It survives for years and years just below the surface. Death cannot kill everything. I've seen mothers fill up with emotion years after the loss of a child. So have you! I've seen grown men, sometimes old men, who couldn't even talk about the death of a parent without becoming visibly distressed.

When Jesus was put to death on the cross, the immediate impact on his disciples must have been devastating. All their hopes and expectations had been crucified with him. It was bad enough that he had been put to death at all, but that he had been subjected to such a degrading and ignominious death was totally demoralising. There was no alternative now but to go back to their homes and pick up the pieces of their original lives. It was easier catch fish than preach failure. Easier take in their nets than take on the Romans. Their movement was finished now. Their cause was lost.

There was more than his broken body buried in the tomb. The coming of the kingdom which he had predicted with such confidence hadn't a hope of engaging them as an objective as long as the King was dead. 'Jesus' end on the cross was not only his private failure but a public catastrophe for his mission.'[1] The King was dead, period. And the kingdom with him. There was no future for Christ's followers in crucifixion.

Where did their future come from? What happened to get them going again? The casualties of Good Friday became the catalysts of a new age. The Christians who had scurried from the cross in disarray and desolation were inexplicably regrouping and showing the kind of dynamism and determination that could hardly owe its impetus to death. Not only were they energising themselves in their local communities, but they were sufficiently motivated to become zealously involved in a world-wide mission, first to the Jews and later to the Gentiles. What was going on? Why was the death of Jesus not doubly lethal? Why did his disciples not continue to mourn him as we continue to mourn our own? There would be no tears in their eyes for Jesus when they would reach old age. What had happened to them?

I had a car outside the back door for some time that would never start in the morning. It wouldn't start at any time! The battery had gone completely flat. Talking to it didn't help at all. Turning the key made no difference. The car wouldn't start without ignition. What ignited the disciples? What kind of experience did they have that put an end to their mourning and changed them as people forever? There has to be an answer and they gave it to us themselves! It lies, of course, in the Resurrection. The New Testament writings all bear witness to that. They tell us, with a single voice, that shortly after his death, the disciples of Jesus declared that God had raised him from the dead and that the risen Jesus himself had commissioned them to proclaim that message to the world. They didn't say they saw him rise. But they did say they saw him risen. St Peter says in the Acts of the Apostles, 'God raised this man Jesus to life ... and all of us are witnesses to that' (Acts 2:32). He says the very same thing in almost the very same words in today's first reading. 'God raised him to life and allowed him to be seen – not by the whole people – but only by certain witnesses ... Now we are those witnesses' (Acts 10:40). And then to drive the point home he adds, 'We have eaten and drunk with him after his Resurrection from the dead' (Acts 10:41). The early disciples are themselves so completely convinced of the reality of the Resurrection that St Paul is prepared to venture everything on its truth. For him, it's the basic, foundational doctrine on which the faith in its entirety depends. 'If Christ has not been raised, then our preaching is useless and your believing is useless' (1 Cor 15:14). Paul was the one who didn't believe at all in the beginning, but who later on incorporated into his first letter to the Corinthians an early and very famous formulation of Resurrection faith which may well have been in use in AD 30, the year Our Lord died. This is what he said: 'Well then in the first place I taught you what I had learned myself, namely that Christ died for our sins in accordance with the scriptures; that he was buried and that he was raised to life on the third day in accordance with the scriptures' (1 Cor 15:3-5). St John gives his own account in today's Gospel – how himself and Peter found only the linen cloths in the empty tomb. Until that moment, he says, 'they had failed to understand the teaching of scripture that he must rise from the dead' (Jn 20:9). The gospel accounts of the Resurrection sometimes differ in detail but the testimony to its truth from all the witnesses is very convincing. People preached the Resurrection and then they died for it. Perhaps the best argument of all comes not from the mouths of the living but from the graves of the dead!

Note
1.   Walter Kasper, *Jesus the Christ*, Paulist Press, 1976, p. 124.

The One We All Need

Acts 5:12-16; Apoc 1:9-13, 17-19; Jn 20:19-31

There is a friend of mine in hospital at the moment who is very, very ill. She has been in and out of hospital now for several years. In recent times her illness has gathered momentum and her own capacity to resist it has steeply declined. She is very weak. I saw her a few days ago but not for long. She's not able for lengthy visits. I hope my visit helped her – but when I left her she was on her own. Her family are wonderful to her, but when they go she's on her own too. The same is true in the case of the medical or nursing staff. They come and go. There's a sense anyway in which we are always on our own. Nobody can live our life for us. We can be helped, but in the living of our own life we cannot be replaced. We live within our own skins – uniquely aware of our own consciousness and the problems that beset us. I cannot live your life for you, or carry the cross that you uniquely bear. No matter how good people are to us, they have to go their own way and live their own lives. No man is an island, as John Donne said, in the sense that we are all responsible for one another. But every man and every woman is an island in that ultimately we have to face the inner reaches, the deeper experiences of life and death on our own. The memories I have from childhood may be similar to those of other people, but they are not exactly the same because every memory is from my own personal perspective. I remember what I remember because I am me. The same is true for you. We are contained within our own consciousness.

The only person who can be with us all the time and know exactly what's going on in our lives is the Lord! And yet there are times – as you know well yourself – when we feel that he's not there at all. I know someone who has prayed for a particular intention for hours and hours every day – for over twenty years – and who is feeling at the end of it all that God is deaf or dead or both.

There were two men on the road to Emmaus – remember them? They were in the depths of despair because they felt Jesus wasn't there, that he was completely absent to them. Yet he was walking by their side step by step! They didn't recognise him until the breaking of the bread. The road to Emmaus is a metaphor for our journey through life. He's walking beside us when we think he's dead.

The disciples in today's Gospel thought he was dead too. They had closed the doors in the room where they were hiding 'for fear of the Jews' (Jn 20:19). They had locked themselves in with their own fears and closed the door on the outside world because, without Jesus, they couldn't cope. They weren't the only ones to close doors. We do it ourselves perhaps at different times and in different ways. If we are young and lacking in confidence, if we are older and lacking in hope, we can withdraw into the cranny of an impoverished, private life. We can be yearning for support, yet unwilling to seek it. A life that was rich in human contact and enthusiasm perhaps becomes increasingly barren and morose. We wait for the knock on the door, yet resent it when it comes. We wait for the phone to ring and go to sleep in the silence. We welcome the recognition that an invitation may bring but return it with excuses. What drives us into isolation may be regret about the past or worry about the future or the death of someone we loved. It may be a hurt with which we cannot cope and from which, at the same time, we're reluctant to part. I knew a man once who became a recluse for life because he suffered a public injustice. He took his hurt with him to the grave and gave it an after-life in his will. People who withdraw into themselves, for whatever reason, need somebody special in their lives to sustain and liberate them. For Christians, that person has to be Jesus. The danger is that in our isolation we may have closed the door on him too. We cannot as Christians live a rounded life on the meagreness of our own resources. We need help from around us – and we should actively seek it – but we also need help from above. 'Jesus came and stood among them,' the Gospel tells us. 'Peace be with you,' he said (Jn 20:19). He freed them from their fear. He even freed Thomas from his doubt. He'll free you from your loneliness too, if you believe in him and make room for him. Don't surrender to isolation! Please open your heart to him and let him bring you his peace.

The Primary Witness

Acts 5:27-32, 40-41; Rom 8:8-17 *or* Apoc 5:11-14;
Jn 14:15-16, 23-26 *or* Jn 21:1-19

Which of the apostles, besides Judas, often gets the poorest press? St Peter I think! It's a bit unfair too because he had an awful lot to recommend him. According to Matthew's Gospel, he was the first, at Caesarea Philippi, to make an act of faith in Jesus as the Christ. 'You are the Christ, the Son of the living God' (Mt 16:16). He was the one too who could work himself up to a passionate declaration of solidarity with Jesus – no matter what the consequences or the cost. 'I would be ready to go to prison with you,' he said, 'and to death' (Lk 22:33). No lack of courage or commitment there. Granted, he made a very bad fist of walking on the water. 'As soon as he felt the force of the wind,' St John tells us, 'he took fright and began to sink' (Jn 14:31). Poor Peter had a tendency to take fright and what sank him, to some extent, in public perception was the way he let Jesus down on the night before his crucifixion at the Palace of Caiphas. He was warming himself at the fire, we are told, when the servant girl challenged him. The fire did nothing for cold feet (Jn 18:18). No, he wasn't a disciple, he insisted, all of three times. The cock crew on his accumulating cowardice and on his remorse and heartbreak as well. Which of us would have done better? Which of us would have said, 'Yes, I am a disciple' and be prepared to face the consequences? We think of Peter in terms of denial in the context of the crucifixion. That's understandable and acceptable provided we have no illusions about ourselves. What we never do is think of Peter in terms of affirmation in the context of resurrection. That's one thing we should be doing. Because if you are looking for the chief witness to the Resurrection of Jesus Christ, St Peter is your man!

The first thing to note is that Peter is named as the primary witness to the Resurrection in some of the earliest formulations of the Christian faith. By formulations, I mean declarations of faith that the early Christians would have made when they'd come together to pray or to celebrate the Eucharist. They'd profess their faith orally of course, and sometimes what they believed would be written down, by preachers for instance. Later on, these professions of faith, or some of them at least, were incorporated into the epistles and Gospels we have. These epistles and Gospels weren't written immediately after the resurrection, but they have long memories. Their roots run very deep. Now at least two of the earliest formulations of resurrection faith make special mention of Peter. The first of these is quoted in Luke's Gospel. 'Yes it is true. The Lord is risen and has appeared to Simon' (Lk 24:34). This, according to the scholars, is a very early acclamation of faith that probably comes from the liturgy. It was something the Christian communities proclaimed and handed on until it found a permanent home, so to speak, in Luke's Gospel. The second formulation of faith that makes mention of Peter is of immense importance. We find it in St Paul's first letter to the people of Corinth. This is what he says: 'I taught you what I had been taught myself, namely, that Christ died for our sins in accordance with the scriptures; that he was buried; that he was raised to life, in accordance with the scriptures; that he appeared first to Cephas and secondly to the twelve … ' (1 Cor 15:3-5).

The wonderful thing about this text, which was handed on to Paul and which he has handed on to us, is that, according to the scholars, it is very, very old. It probably goes back to AD 30, the very year that Jesus rose from the dead. It's thrilling in its immediacy. It brings us as close to the time of the resurrection as we are ever likely to get. In its cadences we hear the living, contemporaneous faith of the resurrection generation. Foremost among the witnesses was the resilient Peter. The force of the wind didn't frighten him every time. He had come a long, long way from the night of his denial.

He's here again in today's readings. And his role as primary witness to Christ's resurrection is further underlined. He is standing up to the Sanhedrin and telling the high priest that he and the apostles are not going to be silenced, because 'obedience to God comes before obedience to men' (Acts 5:29). He throws defiance back in the high priest's face in terms of fact and imputation. 'It was God who raised up Jesus, but it was you who had him executed by hanging on a tree' (Acts 5:30). In the Gospel, when the risen Jesus appeared, Peter didn't try walking on water a second time; he just jumped in (Jn 21:7). It was his impulsive and heartfelt way of bearing witness to his master. Indeed, according to today's Gospel, Peter did far more than believe in the risen Lord; he loved him with all his heart. The faltering follower had become a fervent disciple. Three times he was asked for his love, and three times, in recompense for his denials, he gave it. 'Lord, you know everything. You know that I love you' (Jn 21:17). As Jesus foretold and time would tell, Peter would demonstrate his love for him and 'give glory to God' by the splendour of his witness (Jn 21:19). It would be the supreme irony of his life that he would give the ultimate witness to Christ's resurrection in his own crucifixion. In the reign of Nero, on a date unknown, he was put to death on the cross. As far as we know, they put no inscription on the cross. Had they bothered to do so and had they known his story, the inscription would have read, 'The best placed witness of them all'.

Listening to his Voice

Acts 13:14, 43-52; Apoc 7:9, 14-17; Jn 10:27-30

Some people are very critical of him. Some scholars, I mean. They say he was a very strange man. One scholar wrote that he suffered from 'delusions of persecution and grandeur'.[1] Another described him as 'the first fanatic in the Bible'.[2] A third, taking a much more positive approach, said that, 'he was one of the greatest spiritual figures of all time, in spite of his tendency to abnormality'.[3] Who were they talking about? They were talking about the prophet Ezekiel who is thought to have preached to the Jewish people in both Palestine and Babylon in the sixth century before Christ.

No matter what they say about him and whether it be true or false, there is one passage in the Book of Ezekiel that is absolutely beautiful. It comes in chapter thirty-four. After castigating the wicked shepherds of Israel for neglecting their flock, and feeding themselves rather than their sheep (Ezek 34:3) he quotes the Lord or Yahweh saying this:

> As a shepherd keeps all his flock in view, when he stands up in the middle of his scattered sheep, so shall I keep my sheep in view ... I myself will pasture my sheep, I myself will show them where to rest – it is the Lord Yahweh who speaks – I shall look for the lost one, bring back the stray, bandage the wounded and make the weak strong. I shall watch over the fat and healthy. I shall be a true shepherd to them (Ezek 34:12, 15, 16).

I'm telling you all this because today's Gospel is taken from John, chapter ten, which is largely based on that passage from Ezekiel. Or to put it another way, Jesus built on the passage from Ezekiel to throw light on his own person and mission. And the core of what he is saying is that the shepherding Yahweh promised is being fulfilled in him. He is the 'shepherd of the flock, who calls his sheep one by one and leads them out' (Jn 10:3). He is the Saviour-shepherd who is concerned not only for the flock but for every individual sheep. Changing the image slightly, he then describes himself as 'the gate of the sheepfold' (Jn 10:7). 'Anyone who enters through me will be safe ... and be sure of finding pasture' (Jn 10:9). He is talking about more than grass. He is talking about salvation. He is talking about the highest pastures around – the pastures up in heaven. He spells that out, in very specific terms in verses fourteen and fifteen. 'I am the Good Shepherd ... and I lay down my life for my sheep' (Jn 10:14-15). So the shepherd is not just an ordinary shepherd; he is Saviour, redeemer and, according to today's Gospel, 'one with the Father'. 'The Father and I are one' (Jn 10:30). And because he is all of these things, surely he is entitled to demand a generous response from us when he says, 'The sheep that belong to me listen to my voice. I know them and they follow me' (Jn 10:27).

But do we follow him? Do we listen to his voice? Are we a flock of gentle inoffensive sheep, following our shepherd in spontaneous obedience to his call and in total harmony with each other? Do we not jostle for position at times and butt one another a bit – as ordinary sheep do? Are we as harmless as we look and as well disposed and congenial as we seem? Why are we so eager to tear people to pieces? Why do we behave so wolfishly behind all the cuddly wool?

And apart from the way we knock one another and sometimes do serious harm to one another, do we really listen to Christ's voice as individuals and respond to it as we should? Are we stragglers? Dragging our feet a bit? Keeping in touch with the flock and no more? A sheep will follow the shepherd instinctively. It is not that easy for a human being.

Never easy to respond wholeheartedly to a high moral challenge. The resistance to the call comes from the tangled attachments in our lives. We may respond in spirit to the sound of a call and the heroic character of a summons, but all the elements in our nature aren't equally responsive. Conscience can only go as far as our constitution will allow. If we are lazy, indulgent and just unwilling to be reformed, the insistent calling of the shepherd will go unheeded. In his book, *The Lord*, Romano Guardini puts all this very well when he says: 'Part of me, the profoundest part, listens to it [the shepherd's voice], but superficial, loud contradiction often overpowers it. The opponents with whom God must struggle to win us, are not primarily, the "others" but ourselves; we bar the way. The wolf who puts the hireling to flight is not only outside; he is also within. We are the arch-enemy of our own salvation. And the shepherd must fight first of all with us – for us.'[4] Think about the last remark again. 'The shepherd must fight first of all with us – for us.' I think that's true. So we must will the Lord on, and pray the Lord on and allow him the victory, in every way we can.

Notes
1. See E.C. Broome in Brown, Raymond, *The Jerome Biblical Commentary*, Prentice Hall, 1968, p. 345.
2. Ibid., R.H. Pheiffer.
3. Ibid., Albright.
4. Romano Guardini, *The Lord*, Longmans, 1956, p. 162.

A New Commandment

Acts 14:21-27; Apoc 21:1-5; Jn 13:31-33, 34-35

I want to make the point, just to be awkward, that when Jesus said to his disciples, 'A new commandment I give you ... love one another just as I have loved you' (Jn 13:34), there wasn't that much new about it at all. The notion of 'love', for instance, wouldn't have been new even to the pagan world or, more especially, to Our Lord's disciples. On the contrary, it is a concept with which devout members of the Jewish community would have been familiar. They knew from the Book of Deuteronomy that they should 'love Yahweh their God with all their heart, with all their soul, with all their strength' (Deut 6:4-5). They reminded themselves of that obligation every morning and every night and tried to act on it during the day. They knew from the Book of Leviticus that they were to love their neighbour as themselves (Lev 19:18) and that if they hurt their neighbour they were to repent, make reparation and offer a sacrifice before they could count on God's forgiveness. They knew that love of neighbour extended even to enemy territory. It made its way right up into the front line. Even if they were at war with their enemies, which they often were, love of neighbour forbade them from cutting down the fruit trees on which the enemy depended for survival (Deut 20:19). Not many fruit trees survive in wartime nowadays. The disciples had already heard Jesus putting tremendous emphasis on the importance of loving; when he said that the two greatest commandments were love of God and love of neighbour, 'on these two commandments,' he said, 'hang the whole law and the prophets also' (Mt 22:40). So as inheritors of the Jewish religious tradition and as followers of Jesus himself, the disciples would already have been very conscious of the primacy of love. So what's new?

Most of the newness is in the second part of the new commandment. Jesus didn't merely say 'Love one another'. He said, 'love one another just as I have loved you' (Jn 13:34). Think for a moment of the various elements or strands in that love. Jesus was the Word made flesh (Jn 1:14). His love for all people, including his disciples, had its origins in eternity. It wasn't a sudden emanation. It had been in gestation for a long, long time. Then Jesus had called each one of his disciples by name, not only because he needed them, but more especially because he wanted them. Mark describes that wanting very well in his Gospel when he says, 'He now went up into the hills and he summoned those he wanted so they came to him' (Mk 3:13). For three long years he drew them gradually into his company, weaving them into a fraternity, inspiring them with his teaching, disabusing them of their worldly ambitions, sharing with them on a continuous basis the moods and moments that make for full knowing, experiencing with them, as families do, the heights, the depths and the humdrum of ordinary life. They were a very privileged group. They were in touch with humanity and divinity. They had, in his person, the best of both worlds. Then in the supper room, on the night before his crucifixion, he drew them sacramentally into even closer communion. In fulfilment of the promise made in John, chapter six, he gave them his flesh to eat and his blood to drink (Mk 14:22-25). Then, as if that weren't enough, he did what no slave would do for his master in the culture of the time: he went on his knees before them and washed their feet (Jn 13:5-15). There was no limit to his love for them. They would see it in stripes across his body and in agony against the skyline the following day. The lowering of Holy Thursday would become the emptying of Good Friday. 'His state was divine, yet he did not cling to his equality with God but emptied himself, to assume the condition of a slave ... he was humbler yet, even to accepting death, death on a cross'

(Phil 2:6-8). Jesus himself had the last word on the nature of his love for his disciples when he said, 'A man can have no greater love than to lay down his life for his friends' (Jn 15:13).

Now, I don't think we can match all that but we can try to love people as generously and as faithfully as he did and to do it so well that his influence within us becomes obvious. 'By this love you have for one another,' he said, 'everyone will know that you are my disciples' (Jn 13:35). Two things occur to me straight away. The first is that Christ loves all of us because, as far as he is concerned, each one of us is intrinsically precious. So, the first thing we should give and get in life is justice. If we don't do a decent day's work, for instance, or if we don't get a decent day's pay we are not giving or getting justice. Justice is about giving and getting what is due. So a love that doesn't include justice is not worthy of the name. Love without justice is a hollow thing. Christian love is justice 'warmed up'. If in the home, the workplace and society at large justice doesn't prevail and the dignity of other people is not fully recognised, we are not on Christ's wavelength at all. The second thing that occurs is that the demands of Christian love are not always very considerate. The call to service rarely comes without the tag of inconvenience. We are tired, or we have other plans, or people are looking for too much and the temptation to say 'no' is almost overwhelming. The 'yes' against the tide is a powerful 'yes'. It has the Gospel behind it. Christ seldom said 'no'. He said 'no' to the devil. To pharasaical impositions! To the throwing of stones. All that is true. But he said 'yes' to his Father's will, to people in need and to a terrible inconvenience we call the crucifixion. The more we stand at the foot of the cross the harder it gets to say 'no'. For that reason it has to be a better shadow to stand in than the shadow of our selfish selves.

The Holy Spirit

Acts 15:1-2, 22-29; Apoc 21:10-14, 22-23; Jn 14:23-29

Mike Towey was a great man to tell ghost stories when I was growing up. We were at a wake with him one night and he told us that a coachman went up and down the backways every night, in a coach and four, with his head under his arm and that if he got sight of you (which he could – even with his head the way it was) he'd definitely run you down. He said too that there was a spot in the town down near the bridge, and if you passed it at night a ghost would get you and lead you astray. You could be wandering around for years and years and never make your way home. Mike was right. We knew a house ourselves where a ghost played the piano in the middle of the night – well, not every night because even ghosts get fed up of things, but often enough to draw attention to himself. Oh yes – ghosts were two-a-penny that time, as common as surprise parties are now! And Mike told us – and this is an awful thing – that at a corpse house one night the dead man sat up in the bed and ran the mourners out of the room. Well, he didn't have to run them because they took off themselves! We didn't know what to do, listening to him. If we stayed at the wake the dead man might get up and run us and if we tried to go home the fellow down at the bridge could get us. It was a ghostly dilemma. Would you believe that a few mornings later, when I was on my way in the dark to serve eight o'clock mass, a ghost jumped out from behind a tree in the church grounds. It didn't help to discover later that it was only the sacristan – in a playful mood – with a sheet over him. The next time it happened could be the real thing.

Why am I telling you all this? Well – partly for the fun of it. Partly because it has something to do with the Holy

Spirit. For many of us, the Holy Spirit doesn't figure as much as he should. He's not the real and abiding presence that he ought to be. Maybe it's a problem of visualisation – that we cannot visualise him in human form. God the Father, yes – because we all know what fathers are like, including our own. God the Son, yes too – because we have loved him for years in the person of Jesus. But the Holy Spirit's appearance for us is only symbolic. He is only a breath or the wind or tongues of fire or a dove. The Holy Ghost, (which he used to be), we could picture much better. Ghosts, whenever we saw them or thought we saw them, had much the same shape as ourselves. We could see them. They were there. 'I saw a ghost!' The Holy Spirit isn't there for a lot of us because we cannot get a full-size picture of him at all.

Although we may never visualise him in human shape, I think we might get a better picture of the Holy Spirit if we go for a moment to scripture. There we find how active he is in creation, in the life of Jesus, in the work of the apostles. As for creation, the very first verse in the first book of the Bible tells us, 'the earth was a formless void, there was darkness over the deep and God's spirit hovered over the water' (Gen 1:1-2). The Holy Spirit was there, making order out of chaos. As for the life of Jesus, it was 'through the Holy Spirit' that he was conceived (Mt 1:18); by the Holy Spirit that he was anointed in baptism (Mk 1:10); 'with the power of the spirit' that he carried on his mission (Lk 4:14); 'through the eternal spirit' that he offered himself on the cross (Heb 9:14) and 'in the order of the spirit' that he was raised from the dead (Rom 1-4). As for the work of the apostles, Jesus promised in today's Gospel that the Holy Spirit would be of enormous assistance to them. 'The Advocate, the Holy Spirit, whom the Father will send in my name, will teach you everything and remind you of all I have said to you' (Jn 14:26). He proved himself a worthy advocate as we saw in the first reading. When some people were insisting that the Jewish practice of circumcision should be a requirement for membership of the Church, the Holy Spirit and the apostles decided otherwise. He was on that occasion, as on many other occasions, in the right place at the right time.

He's there for you now at this very moment. He's there for me. Do you know one of the reasons why we cannot pin him down pictorially? He's too busy, too active, a kind of divine blur! He is so many different things: counsellor; comforter; invigorator; friend. If one could say it without offence – he's the life and soul of the Trinity. And we need him in all his roles. Life for all of us is a hazardous experience. We have choices to make and don't know which way to go. We have made our mistakes and must live with our remorse. We are stricken with disease and aren't sure that we'll survive. We have lost the love of our life and are desolate on our own. No Spirit, however holy, will solve all these things for us. He'll need to put humans in our way as well. But he will help! And he's waiting to help. There are more coachmen out there ready to run us down and more ghosts to lead us astray than we ever dreamed. But there's a God out there too, the depth of whose kindness we haven't dreamed of either. Let's draw him into the needy parts of our life in the fullness of the Holy Spirit.

THESE MIGHT HELP TOO

Not Gone At All

Acts 1:1-11; Eph 1:17-23 *or* Heb 9:24-28; Lk 24:46-53

The impression we could easily derive from St Luke's description of the Ascension in the first reading and Gospel is that Jesus had departed for good; he was there one minute and abruptly gone the next. In the first reading, the apostles were hoping that he would stay around, get down to business and 'restore the Kingdom to Israel' (Acts 1:5). But, before they knew it, they were standing with their mouths open, looking up at the sky. We nearly get the impression that Our Lord was in a hurry. The Gospel says that 'as he blessed them' – in the middle of blessing them so to speak – 'he was carried up to heaven' (Lk 24:51). The impression that he has gone for good has all the finality of a curtain coming across in the theatre or a door closing in your face. Even while the apostles looked up, wondering what on earth was going on, they found themselves separated from him by a cloud. They had seen all they were going to see – and that was that! 'A cloud took him from their sight' (Acts 1:9).

Is that what St Luke is saying to us? That Jesus is gone for good? That everything is over? A cloud drawn under Our Lord's feet as opposed to a line? I believe he tells us the opposite. What he is really saying can be summed up in two sentences. Jesus was there for us then. Jesus is there for us now. Jesus was there for us then, but in what sense? He was there in the last of his Easter appearances, as the risen and exalted Christ. We are not familiar with the notion of exaltation. It means that not only was Jesus raised from the dead, he was also raised on high. He was invested with kingly power as Lord of the universe. As far as St John was concerned, Jesus was exalted even on the cross. His cross was more than a cross, it was also a throne from which he reigned as Saviour and drew mankind to himself. 'And when I am lifted up from the earth,' Jesus had said, 'I will draw all men to myself' (Jn 12:32). So there was triumph in the cross – and exaltation – where onlookers could see only failure! Where St Matthew and St Paul were concerned, Jesus was exalted in his resurrection. He wasn't merely a risen figure – as Lazarus was – he was a uniquely authoritative figure as well. The risen Christ could say, as Matthew quotes him as saying, 'All authority in Heaven and on earth has been given to me. Go therefore and make disciples of all the nations' (Mt 28:18-19). You can feel the power going out of Jesus, the dominance of his presence, the ascendancy of his truth. St Luke is very conscious of all that in today's readings. Jesus tells the apostles, 'You will receive power when the Holy Spirit comes on you'; 'You will be my witnesses not only in Jerusalem but to the ends of the earth' (Acts 1:8). And it is because Luke is so conscious of how highly exalted Christ is as the resurrected Lord that he describes him in the Ascension as 'lifted up' (Acts 1:9) and 'carried up to heaven' (Lk 24:51). This person that Luke and the others describe for us is majestic in his person, in his drawing power, in his triumph over death, in his authority, in his mission. He was there for the apostles in all of those ways, in his risen appearances, including his last. He was there for us too. If he seemed in his Ascension to go in a hurry or to be gone forever, he left some legacy.

If he was there for us then – and he was – then Jesus is there for us yet. Despite the impression we get from Luke that he went zooming into the heavens, he went no distance at all. What the Ascension means is that Jesus withdrew from human sight to be with the Father. The preface in today's mass reminds us that Jesus went to heaven 'not to abandon us, but to be our hope'. St Paul reminds us constantly that Jesus is with the Father as our intercessor. 'At God's right hand,' he says, 'he stands and pleads for us'

THESE MIGHT HELP TOO

(Rom 8:34). That was in his letter to the Romans. He repeats the same message several times in his letter to the Hebrews. 'He's our supreme high priest,' he says, 'who has gone through to the highest heaven' (Heb 4:14). 'Christ,' he tells us again, 'is in the actual presence of God on our behalf' (Heb 9:24). It couldn't be plainer than that. And what's immensely consoling is that he is not there in a subordinate position, so to speak. He is not there merely as intercessor, to put in a word for us. He is there as *the* Word himself, as the exalted one, enthroned on high. Jesus shares in divine power. St Peter reminds us that 'he has made the Angels and Dominations and Powers his subjects' (1 Pet 3:22). It is from that position of power – the position of shared divinity – that he intercedes on our behalf. According to St Paul, Christ's 'power to save is utterly certain, since he is living forever to intercede for all who come to God through him' (Heb 7:25).

I know now, and so do you, that one of the greatest blessings you could have in life is a faithful friend, somebody who will always stand by you and do anything for you. We all need someone to turn to when our inner resources are running low, someone to be with, someone who will enjoy the good times and pull us through the difficult times. The best alternative medicine in life is friendship. Pal-ology. It is great to feel comfortable in someone's company, to know that you are accepted for what you are, to be free to speak openly about how you are feeling, to know that your back is safe and that you are not going to be criticised or shafted as soon as you go out the door. The confidence of friendship. We all enjoy or can enjoy that kind of friendship with Christ. We all have the best friend in the world in the highest of places. And we can trust him to the last. He is not just ready to give us his friendship, he is actually looking for ours – canvassing ours! 'I shall not call you servants any more [...] I call you friends' (Jn 15:15). 'Come to me, all you who labour and are overburdened and I will give you rest' (Mt 11:28). We are foolish if we don't come to him, impoverished if we don't come to him, because not only is he our friend – he is our salvation. I hope that no matter how indifferent or sinful we may have been in the past, we'll come closer to Jesus now. And in Jesus to God. There is no better way. We have no better friend. What we've been saying in today's homily is true. In his final Easter appearance and in his Ascension, Jesus was there for us then and he's there for us now!

A Sense of Purpose

Acts 2:1-11; Rom 8:8-17 *or* 1 Cor 12:3-7, 12-13;
Jn 14:15-16, 23-26 *or* Jn 20:19-23

I may be wrong, but I don't think today's feast means that much to most people. If we are told it is important, we'll take it on faith, but we don't really feel it. It doesn't get into the blood like Christmas or Easter or even smaller feasts like Halloween. For one thing, the word 'Pentecost' has no immediacy in terms of meaning. It's a word from somebody else's vocabulary – a puzzling survival from another age. In addition to that, the Holy Spirit himself is tantalizingly insubstantial. The symbols that we associate with him like wind or fire or breath or dove, while powerfully appropriate in themselves, have nothing like the appeal of a baby in a manger. It's very difficult, even for the Holy Spirit, to compete with the incarnation. The most disturbing thing of all, I think, is that the account of the Spirit's coming in the Acts of the Apostles stretches our credulity. So many unlikely things happening all at once. A fireworks display of the miraculous. Wind in their ears. Tongues of fire on their heads. Foreign languages at their beck and call! It's not the real world as we know it. Even by the standards of the miraculous it seems to be well over the top!

The first thing we need to understand is that the coming of the Holy Spirit was an interior experience. It was an experience of soul and heart and mind. And that spiritual experience was so intense that in order to externalise it for his readers, St Luke felt compelled to describe it in terms of movement and image and sound. The Holy Spirit came in fact. He also came in metaphor. He came like the wind, lifting them up, carrying them along, propelling them onwards. He does it for us too. He is the wind on our backs, the help we need over hills, the little push we need when we're stalling. He is the fire in our lives as well, in the enthusiasm he engenders, the warmth he imparts, the evil he isolates and destroys. For all the energy he generates and the fury of wind and fire, there is no violence in his coming. He comes to us not in the swoop of the hawk but in the gentleness of the dove. He comes with a universal message too. That's the significance of the speaking in foreign tongues. The Good News is for all people. The Gospel is to be internationalised. Just as our Lord's mission began with the descent of the Spirit at his baptism, so the preaching mission of the Church begins with the descent of the Spirit at Pentecost. It's a time to be up and doing. In the life of the apostles, in the life of the infant Church, a new era has begun.

So what's the message of Pentecost for us? Well, you know yourself that the most remarkable thing about the coming of the Holy Spirit was the enormous impact he made on the disciples of Jesus. He literally changed them for life. He took a group of people who were cowering behind closed doors, shook the timidity out of them and gave them the courage to put their lives on the line. Will hares turn round and face the hounds? Well, with the Holy Spirit to stand behind them, that's what the disciples did. Where fear had reigned, fortitude took over. The greatest gift the Holy Spirit gave the disciples was a bit of backbone. Led by Peter, whose back had given him trouble on an earlier occasion, they stood up straight, faced a formidable crowd and preached Christ crucified and risen. 'God raised this man Jesus to life,' Peter told them, 'and all of us are witnesses to that' (Acts 2:32). They had found their voices, rediscovered their vocation, embarked on their mission. They had been raised to life by the Spirit.

Our message for Pentecost is in their example. We need to be raised to life too – to a new level of commitment. Pentecost is about enthusiasm, about momentum, about a courageous missionary spirit. It's not a time for hiding behind closed doors – even if all we have on the other side of the door is apathy or indifference. It's a time to be fired up a bit, to be conscious of the wind at our backs. Lent and Pentecost have something in common. They are both related to spring. Lent, unfortunately, tends to have a narrow focus in terms of renewal. Many people focus on one or two particulars, like giving up drink or cigarettes. Pentecost is a time for a broader vision, a time for an in-depth assessment of our lives as Christians, a time to discern and decide. The problem for the disciples, before Pentecost, is that they were lacking in backbone. Could the problem for us be that we have grown flabby? Well-meaning but ineffectual? Letting things drift – especially on the devotional side; careless about Sunday mass, sacraments, prayer in the home, a middle-aged faith that has lost its youthful fitness? Give it a thought. We are meant to be Pentecostal people. To have a sense of purpose. If our faith happened to bump into somebody, would the other person be conscious of a collision? As inheritors of an explosive beginning and a history of missionary endeavour, we don't have the right to be casual. He is our Holy Spirit too.

Ordinary

Time

A People's Person

Is 62:1-5; 1 Cor 12:4-11; Jn 2:1-11

The Canon, as we called him, was one lovely man. From a child's point of view, he was the kind of person a grown man should be. He'd clap his hands at a distance when you'd be stealing apples from his orchard to make sure that you'd get away. He'd visit the school every now and again at lunchtime and walk up and down the footpath with the teachers so that we'd be left with a longer break for play. His thanksgiving after Mass was a mixture of prayers and pennies, prayers to the God he served and pennies to those of us who served him. When the Mass was over and the vestments had been benched, he'd turn his back on our expectations, only heightening them all the more. He'd rummage in his trousers pocket, raising the possibility that he was penniless at last and then turn round reassuringly with the coppers in his hand. He was so dependable. He was telling us in his wonderfully predictable way that we were never far from his mind. When Saturdays came round we besieged him in the Confessional. We hemmed him in with our sins and had complete confidence in his compassion. He was a great man with people, was our Canon. He was a people's person. There is hardly a day goes by that he doesn't come warmly into my mind. Others of my generation remember him in the same way. He was foundational in our lives – living proof that, to some extent anyway, the world was built on benevolence. He had within him the kindness that lasts. The patriot dead are not the only ones who speak to us from their graves. The pastoral dead speak to us too in words that only the heart can hear.

If our Canon, as a disciple of Jesus, was a people's person, then in that regard he was only trotting after his

Master. Jesus of Nazareth had to be the greatest people's person of all time. His feeling for people comes across with tremendous power in the passage from Isaiah that he chose as his public manifesto. We will meet it again in next Sunday's Gospel. 'The Spirit of the Lord has been given to me, for he has anointed me. He has sent me to bring good news to the poor, to proclaim liberty to captives and to the blind new sight, to set the downtrodden free, to proclaim the Lord's year of favour' (Lk 4:18, 19). He would spend the rest of his public ministry doing precisely that. Nobody lived up to his commitments as thoroughly as did Jesus. The number of healings attributed to him in the Gospel for instance, over a very short period, is quite extraordinary. What is equally extraordinary is not just the healing touch but the time he had for the individual person. There is no hint of the whirl-wind campaign here – the wave for one, the wink for anoth-er, the hug for a third. The impression we get is that with everyone who crossed his path, Jesus had a genuine encounter. Everyone he met mattered to him, immediately, deeply and eternally. We have only to think about the woman at the well for instance (Jn 4:5-26) or the centurion with the sick servant (Mt 8:5-13) or the paralytic they let down through the roof (Mt 9:18). And if Jesus had a prefer-ence for one group of people rather than another, it was for those who had been marginalised by the rich or the right-eous and who recognised that their greatest spiritual need in life was for forgiveness. That much is made clear in the parable of the Pharisee and the Publican alone (Lk 18:9-14). Not that Jesus excluded anybody. If people stayed outside his circle it was because they excluded themselves. Even as he hung upon the cross he brought the people who had just crucified him within the scope of his dying embrace! 'Father forgive them; they do not know what they are doing' (Lk 23:34). He knew well what he was doing, though. He had been doing it all his life. The only harvesting that mattered to him was a harvesting of single grains.

I haven't departed from today's Gospel. The changing of the water into wine is part of the pattern I've been talking about. It was Our Lord's first miracle and it was done for people. For the couple, for their parents, for the guests, for his mother. It was done for life, for celebration, for enjoyment. And the changing of the water into wine had a wider significance – a symbolic significance. Whoever tasted the wine first tasted the future Christ would bring – in this life and the life to come. Where there was sin he would bring forgiveness; where there was darkness he would bring light; where there was ignorance, he would bring truth; where there was death he would bring resurrection. The wine is the presence of Jesus in our midst – the wine that brings colour to our watery existence. The wine is the new way, the new faith, the new future, that we have all inherited and that we take so much for granted. We must raise our glasses today to the Saviour in our midst, not to his health, but to his great love for us, to all he has done for us. If the Canon was foundational in our lives as children, how much more so is Jesus? In his living and in his dying have we not proof of his benevolence? If our God is a God for people, aren't we a miserable lot entirely if we do not try to live and love our faith?

Jesus was Different

Neh 8:2-6, 8-10; 1 Cor 12:12-30; Lk 1:1-4, 4:14-21

We get used to things. Very used to things! Used to the shrine being down there. To the Ambo being here – it used to be over there. To the colour around the window being white. Do you remember what colour it used to be? When we get used to things they lose their initial impact – the impact they made on us when we saw them for the first time. I'm just wondering if we haven't got used to Jesus.

The reason I say that is because in his own time Jesus of Nazareth was a most unusual person. He was a shocker! A troubling, disconcerting figure. He still is. Listen as if for the first time to some of the things he said. 'Love your enemies. Do good to those who hate you. Bless those who curse you. Pray for those who treat you badly' (Lk 6:27-28). Is that what we hear? Is that what we do? It's what he did even in the agony of crucifixion. 'Father, forgive them – they do not know what they are doing'. He was very different.

Take another example. Who did Jesus mix with? Holy people? Some of the time. But certainly not all of the time. He mixed with people on the edge, outcasts, those whom his own people considered unclean. He broke the social code when everybody expected him to keep it. He even broke the Jewish Sabbath when he was required to heal. So different was his behaviour that he was pilloried by his critics as a glutton and a drunkard (Mt 11:19). He even went so far as to socialise with tax collectors who weren't among the downtrodden at all but who were themselves exploiters –collecting taxes for the Romans and additional ones for themselves. Many of his own people must have hated Jesus for that – for including the collaborator and the corrupt in his circle. What they couldn't understand is that God is a people's God, a God for all sorts, a God whose love and salvation is offered unconditionally to everybody, provided, of course, that they repent and believe. As far as the pious Jews were concerned, if God was a God for all sorts, then he couldn't be holy.[1] This revolutionary new message about the nature and attitude of God had to be coming from a false prophet. There was only one penalty in Jewish law for being a false prophet and that penalty was death (Deut 18:20). Being a false prophet would translate for the Romans into political rebel. And it was for being a rebel that they crucified him. There was a certain inevitability about the crucifixion of Jesus. It was in his claims and in his character. When all is said and done, it was in his blood.

You get another example of the difference in him – the originality – in today's Gospel. Even John the Baptist, who introduced him to the world, was astonished by what Jesus had to say. John the Baptist was a tough man. He'd really put the skids under you, and in a voice that could be heard all over the desert. His was the word of God amplified. Jesus began his own mission on the same note as John – if not the same volume. He said, 'Repent, for the kingdom of Heaven is close at hand' (Mt 4:17). But then – and this is important – Jesus embarked on a ministry of his own. Whereas John the Baptist was all fire and brimstone – 'the axe is laid to the roots of the trees' (Mt 3:10) – the emphasis from Jesus is on God's burning love. The attitude he adopted was so different from John's. You have it in today's Gospel in the words he quoted from the prophet Isaiah: 'The Spirit of the Lord has been given to me – for he has anointed me – to bring the good news to the poor [...] to proclaim liberty to captives – and to the blind new sight – to set the downtrodden free [...] to proclaim the Lord's year of favour' (Lk 4:18-19). What is noticeable about this passage is the gentleness of the tone and the positive nature of the content. If sinners are in his sights, they are not there to be shot at but to be saved. The people he mentions and whom he means to liberate are all captives of one kind or another. They have been axed in life enough already without being axed by him again. 'The joy of the Lord is their stronghold' (Neh 8:10), rather than the fire of chastisement their fate. Whereas in John's case, God's rule of the world would be marked by judgement and punishment and retribution, in the case of Jesus it would be marked by judgement, yes, but even more so by compassion and understanding and love. Anybody reading the early part of the script could predict what he'd say to the woman in adultery. It was nothing if not in character. 'Neither do I condemn you, go away, and don't sin any more' (Jn 8:11).

There is a picture of Our Lady hanging in the porch. I asked the children in school about it one day. They couldn't describe it. Didn't remember seeing it. They hadn't really noticed it. Do we pass by the person of Jesus without really noticing? Without really noticing the extraordinary nature of his teaching – and the way he behaved. Loving enemies, praying for persecutors, having time for the outcasts in society, the pariahs, being actively concerned about the poor, the sick and the disabled. Let's not get too used to Jesus. There's comfort in him of course. But there is also one heck of a challenge. If he doesn't shock us at times and shake us out of our lethargy, we really don't know him at all.

Note
1. See Walter Kasper, *Jesus the Christ,* Paulist Press, 1976, p. 67.

Sharing in his Mission

Jer 1:4-5, 17-19; 1 Cor 12:31-13; Lk 4:21-30

Do you know what we do very often with the first reading? We park it! Or if you want to change the image a little, we treat it like an official driver is sometimes treated. We leave it sitting outside in the car without bringing it within the ambit of our consideration. We are not sufficiently familiar with it to embrace it in the same way as we embrace the Gospel! It is there, known to be there, given public recognition, but subsequently ignored. Not always of course, but as a general rule!

We certainly shouldn't ignore it on this occasion because it's an ideal introduction to today's Gospel. It strikes a chord that the Gospel will subsequently take up and amplify. There are resonances in both passages of a similar kind. The mission of Jeremiah foreshadows what would happen in the mission of Christ. One of the difficulties Jeremiah would have to encounter was opposition. This would come from his own people, the people of Judah, during the very turbulent period of 626–587 BC. He would witness the clash between two great empires, the result of which would be the predominance of the Babylonian over the Assyrian. He would see the downfall of the kingdom of Judah and the destruction of its capital, Jerusalem. He would see the people of Judah deported by the Babylonians until only the 'poor of the land' were left. His task in life was to preach God's love for Judah and warn of impending catastrophe should Judah fail to return the love of God. The second part of his message, condemning his people for their apostasy, proved a difficult lesson for the people. Hence his awareness of their opposition in today's reading. He talks about 'bracing himself for action' (Jer 1:17); about having to 'confront the Kings of Judah and its princes' (Jer 1:18); about the vehemence with which they would 'fight against him' (Jer 1:19). He was one of their own. Yet the people of Judah wouldn't listen to him. He wouldn't be the first to find himself in that situation and as today's Gospel makes clear to us, he wouldn't be the last.

Jesus says in today's Gospel: 'this text is being fulfilled today even as you listen' (Lk 4:21). The text he is talking about is the one from Isaiah that we read last Sunday (and the Sunday before), predicting the coming of the Messiah and the nature of his kingdom. 'The Spirit of the Lord has been given to me; for he has anointed me. He has sent me to bring the good news to the poor, to proclaim liberty to captives and to the blind new sight, to set the downtrodden free, to proclaim the Lord's year of favour' (Lk 4:18-19). Initially what Jesus had to say seems to have been well received by the Nazarenes. But in the midst of the applause, somebody must have started the slow handclap. We hear it in our local communities sometimes when one of our own does too well. Begrudgery is not happy with ascensions. Carpenters' sons are always permitted to make rungs for others but never for themselves. Once they have the neck to start climbing above their origins, your duty is to grab and pull them down. Begrudgery at Nazareth became toxic entirely when mixed with envy of Capernaum. Why all the miracles in that place and no miracle in their place at all? They were simmering with resentment at this stage. It was when Jesus indicated that his mission would not be confined to Jewish people, but would be inclusive of pagan peoples as well, as the mission of Elijah and Elisha had been, that resentment boiled over in fury. They would drag this upstart to the only height to which he was entitled to aspire and send him plunging to the fate that he deserved! The 'brow of the hill' to which they dragged him is, in St Luke's mind, a foreshadowing of the Hill of Calvary (Lk 4:29). This fury that Jesus had stirred up would never really

THESE MIGHT HELP TOO

abate. It would erupt again in Jerusalem in the final attempt to destroy him on the cross. Luke is suggesting to us that this attempt too would fail. Death would find him even more elusive than the Nazarenes had. He would slip through the chains and 'walk away' from death in his resurrection and ascension (Lk 4:30).

Hasn't there been enough opposition in today's readings to God's word and the Word made flesh without our adding to it? What side do we want to be on anyway? Since the mission of Jesus is extended to the whole wide world, including ourselves, shouldn't we be doing our best to live his love and pass it on to others? And because Isaiah's text is fulfilled in his person, what better way to live his love than 'to bring good news to the poor, proclaim liberty to captives and set the downtrodden free' (Lk 4:18-19). And the poor are not just the materially poor. They are the sick, the bereaved, the moral rejects of a self-righteous world and those whose knowledge of Jesus is meagre or non-existent. The captives will include ourselves too – slaves as we are – to selfishness and sin. They will include those in the armlock of addiction, as well as a member of our family or our community perhaps whom we might be able to help. There are all sorts of situations where the downtrodden can be helped or set free. One thing is for sure. We have no business dragging Jesus to 'the brow of a hill in order to throw him down the cliff' (Lk 4:30). Our job is to climb the highest hill we can find to help him up in the shape of his people. We are privileged as Christians to share in his mission and to help stoke a fire that will never go out.

Teaching that is New

Is 6:1-8; 1 Cor 15:1-11; Lk 5:1-11

We grew up between two giants, my generation and the previous generation. We grew up between two powerful figures who dominated our consciousness and divided our loyalties. I'm talking about Éamon de Valera and Michael Collins. One was alive and well and celebrated in the public arena; the other was tragically dead, yet deathless in the public memory. No two Irishmen, since Daniel O'Connell and later Parnell, had such an overwhelming impact on their respective followers. Both men were different but similarly charismatic. Both enjoyed legendary status even when they were still young men. There are people alive even today who would certainly give their first vote and maybe their last breath for Éamon de Valera and Michael Collins. Whether you were for them or against them, one thing these two had in common was the capacity to inspire devotion. They captivated people, energised people, kept them in thrall. Those who supported one or the other always looked up.

I mention that now because in all three readings today you have that element of unconditional devotion. There is a huge difference of course in that, as regards Éamon de Valera and Michael Collins, it was devotion to mere mortals (even though some might not agree), whereas in the case of Isaiah, Paul and Simon it was devotion to the Divinity, to the God above and his Son below. In the first reading the prophet Isaiah commits himself totally to the God of Israel. Having had his speech refined in the fire of an angel's touch, he expressed his willingness to serve God as messenger. 'Here I am,' he proclaimed, 'send me' (Is 6:8). In the second reading, having encountered the risen Christ on the road to

THESE MIGHT HELP TOO

Damascus, St Paul was so enthralled by the encounter, so graced by it, that in his own words, 'he had worked harder than any of the other' apostles (I Cor 15:10). And in the Gospel, Simon Peter is so overwhelmed by the person of Christ, by his words and works that, like the two sons of Zebedee, 'he leaves everything and follows him' (Lk 5:11). What's being emphasised in the first reading is God's impact on Isaiah. What's emphasised in the second reading is Christ's impact on St Paul. What's central to the Gospel is the enormous impression Christ made on Simon. What all three experienced was transformation. They would never be the same again. So overpowered and humbled were they by these encounters with pure goodness that all three of them felt unworthy and unclean. Simon, for instance, said, 'Leave me Lord; I am a sinful man' (Lk 5:8). Political leaders, whatever their strengths, don't make us feel sinful. They will draw loyalty out of us but not remorse, protestations of fealty but not confession. The change that Jesus brought about in Paul and Simon was fundamentally moral. He touched the best in them and made them conscious of the worst. They had found not just a leader but a saviour too. They weren't asked, like supporters, to give him their first vote – their number one. What they did give him, as martyrs, was their last breath.

What today's readings urge is that you and I do the same – give him our last breath! Not necessarily die for him, but give ourselves unreservedly to him, as Paul and Simon did, whatever the consequences. And in the interests of brevity, I'll suggest just one reason why we should do that. It hasn't to do directly, as it could, with his compassion, his love for us, his dying on the cross, even his resurrection. It has to do with an apparently cold but very important thing – his authority. Who he was! Who he is! We live, as you know, in an increasingly relativist age. And the relativist mentality would say that one prophet is as good as another – a kind of a 'pick your prophet' approach. I had a discussion with a friend of mine recently who insisted that the authority of Jesus was no greater than that of Moses, Jeremiah or Mohammed or anyone else. That's not what Jesus said himself. Far from it. That's not what his hearers said about him. When he first appeared on the scene his contemporaries knew he was different. Very different! They knew that what he was saying was astounding. 'Here is a teaching that is new,' they said, 'and with authority behind it' (Mk 1:27). The authority behind it and to which he laid claim, believe it or not, was the authority of God. As far as the Jewish people were concerned, the highest authority who spoke for God was their Moses. This Jesus placed himself way above Moses. He was claiming to be the highest peak – even higher than Mount Sinai! What had come from God, through previous prophets – important though it was – was not the final word. He was the final word. That's what he was saying! He would say things like, 'it was said to the men of old' – 'but I say to you!' (Mt 5:22, 28, 34). He was laying claim to an authority that was unique. He put it another way when he claimed to forgive sin (Mt 9:2). He put it another way still when, according to Matthew's Gospel, he said to the Scribes and Pharisees 'there is something greater than Jonah here'; 'there is something greater than Solomon here' (Mt 12:41-2). Jesus made no bones about his authority and his listeners understood him so well and were so shocked by the implications of what he was saying that they could come to only one conclusion. 'He is blaspheming' (Mk 2:7). He was making himself equal to God. They had him crucified for it in the end because they couldn't handle it at all. So it's not a question of 'pick your prophet'. All of them have a great deal to offer. Of course they do. But only one of them should have the primary place in our hearts and lives because only one of them is the Son of God.

Happy are You who are Poor

Jer 17:5-8; 1 Cor 15:12, 16-20; Lk 6:17, 20-26

I don't mean to be smart, but how happy are you with the 'happies' in today's Gospel? Happy the poor, the hungry, the weeping and the persecuted. What have they to be happy about? It's puzzling to say the least. As a matter of fact, I think many of us listen to the Beatitudes with great attention and appreciation, without having much of an idea at the end as to what they mean. The sound of them comes easier than the sense. The point of them often gets lost in the paradox. Luke has Jesus saying, 'How happy are you who are poor' (Lk 6:20), and those of us who are strapped for cash or struggling to pay the mortgage cannot see much to be happy about. People who are poor might be happy in spite of it. But why should they be happy because of it? Is Jesus telling us that the way to be completely happy is to have nothing at all?

No, he's not. He's not celebrating poverty or endorsing it. He's not endorsing hunger either. The whole thrust of the Gospel message is towards the elimination of both. Helping the poor and hungry is of such personal concern to Jesus that what we do for them, we do for him. So he said himself: 'I was hungry and you gave me food. I was thirsty and you gave me drink ... naked and you clothed me' (Mt 25:35-36). If concern for the poor wasn't a Gospel requirement or imperative, then the rich man Lazarus, who ignored the poor man on his doorstep, wouldn't have found himself, in Our Lord's story, down in the depths of hell (Lk 16:19-31). No, Jesus is on the side of the poor. This is what Luke is emphasising in today's Gospel. He is not antagonistic to the rich but his preference is for those who have little or nothing. After all, he was one of them himself. In the Greek and Jewish tradition, the man who was blessed by God or thought to be blessed by God would be long in years and never short of a shekel. The man who was well preserved and well heeled was thought to be 'well in' with 'the man above'! Jesus puts a different slant on that perception. The God he knew was in nobody's pocket. The people who were 'blessed by God', and described as such by Jesus, were not the propertied but the poor. And among the poor were those who were persecuted on his account. The reason all the poor are blessed is that he has come to be their liberator and Saviour and to invite them to be citizens of his kingdom. No other earthly blessing could ever compare with that. To be one with him and with one another is the greatest blessing of all. In order to inherit the kingdom, of course the poor need to have the right attitude. They need to have the humility or 'poverty of spirit' that Matthew emphasises in his Beatitudes (Mt 5:3). That kind of poverty is not confined to any particular class. It can be found right across the social spectrum from the poorest to the wealthiest! All of us are beggars before God. There is a hole in every pocket. It's important to realise that. 'How happy are you who are poor' (Lk 6:20).

There aren't too many 'happies' in the second part of today's Gospel. In fact, there is none at all! What we get instead are the 'four woes'! 'Woe to you' or 'alas for you' who are rich, sated, smug in your superfluity and feted by the world (Lk 6:24-26). Is this an assault on prosperity, on tigers, celtic and otherwise, on the comfortable lifestyle that many people enjoy and to which most people aspire? No, it's not! It's two things. First of all, as we have seen, it's a rejection of the traditional Greek and Jewish belief that the more you had, the more you enjoyed God's favour. And secondly, it's a warning to the rich not to become entangled in the briars of their own prosperity, not to fall victim to the poverty of their own greed. It's another way of saying, 'How happy are the poor in spirit' (Mt 5:3). How happy are those who recognise the value of sharing and the richness of human dependency on the God above. It's also an echo of what Jeremiah said in the first reading. 'A curse on the man ... who relies on things of flesh' (Jer 17:5). 'A blessing on the man who puts his trust in the Lord' (Jer 17:7).

So, what we are seeing today is Jesus putting in the foundations of a new kingdom; supplying the blocks or the solid and substantial values on which the kingdom is to be built. Values like humility, trust in God, a hunger for his word, a willingness to share, a readiness to suffer and endure. At the same time, what we are seeing is Jesus shaking the foundations of an older and uglier kingdom where greed and self indulgence hold sway. As a matter of fact, in a book entitled *The Shaking of the Foundations*,[1] Paul Tillich sums up today's Gospel in two powerful sentences: 'Jesus praises the poor in so far as they live in two worlds, the present world and the world to come. And he threatens the rich in so far as they live in one world alone.' The lesson for us, whether we be rich or only aspiring to riches, is not to live in one world alone.

Note

1. Paul Tillich, *The Shaking of the Foundations*, Penguin, 1969, p. 36.

Love Your Enemies

1 Sam 26:2, 7-9, 12-13, 22-23; 1 Cor 15:45-49; Lk 6:27-38

I think we should begin with God. Not a bad place to begin! He wasn't a begrudger. He didn't have it in for us. He didn't say to himself, 'I'll let them stew in their own juice'. No! No! 'God loved the world so much that he gave his only Son, so that everyone who believes in him may not be lost but may have eternal life' (John 3:16). Matthew says in his Gospel that God's love is indiscriminate. 'For he causes his sun to rise on bad men as well as good and his rain to fall on honest and dishonest men alike' (Mt 5:45). God's love is always on the look out! Always searching the horizon. Looking for dots in the distance. Narrowing its eyes against the evening sun. The Prodigal Son didn't come home unawares. He came on God the Father's watch. God's love went running to meet him. If God has enemies amongst us, he doesn't let on.

I think we should continue with Jesus. Not one to fall out with his friends even when they let him down. To be let down once would be bad enough but to be let down three times in the course of an evening, when he needed support most! But he didn't dispense with Peter. He made him the rock on which he'd build his Church. The cock crowed that morning not just on denial but on forgiveness. On a new day! Not one to fall out with his enemies either. Even when they had subjected him with their customary savagery to the indignity and horror of Crucifixion, he said: 'Father, forgive them, they do not know what they are doing' (Lk 23:34).

I think we should consider ourselves, in a general way at first. When Jesus began his mission and inaugurated his kingdom, the condition of membership was conversion. The

THESE MIGHT HELP TOO

old ways had to be abandoned and a new set of values embraced. 'Repent,' he said (or be converted), 'the kingdom of heaven is close at hand' (Mt 4:17). The most important value in that new set of values is an unselfish and indiscriminate love, a love that extends, not just to family and friends, but even to enemies, or those we regard as enemies. The kingdom is a new departure – a new way. It is meant to break down barriers and eliminate prejudices, personal, racial and religious. It is meant to uproot in man the primitive urges for strike and retaliation, to put an end to the senseless circles of violence and counter violence that still disfigure our world. When you consider the havoc that is caused by hatred, the devastation in streets and human hearts, love of enemies doesn't seem that far fetched at all. It is a Christian injunction that is immensely practical in its consequences. I think John Hume has worked for it all his political life. Nelson Mandela worked for it in South Africa when, after twenty-seven years in jail, he made peace and a political future with his enemies. There is no future in hate. There is a future – and the prospect of peace and justice – in the practice of love.

Finally, I think we should apply love of enemies to our own local situation. Do you recall what happened in the first reading? Saul was King of Israel and David was at war with him. While Saul was asleep David could have pinned him to the ground with his own spear. He wouldn't do it! Was that to his credit? Oh, I think it was. It will be to our credit too if we don't use the spear to pin anybody. We may make enemies in life – unfortunately – but we don't have to keep them. We can let the enmity go, on our side anyway. Protect our interests, yes, but let the enmity go! That's what Jesus is saying to us. 'Do good to those who hate you; bless those who curse you, pray for those who treat you badly' (Lk 6:27). I met a person lately who had been very deeply hurt by another and who had suffered a great deal of pain as a result. There was a huge temptation there to take revenge. The one who had been hurt was the one who was most willing to forgive. I couldn't get over it. I haven't met a human being for years who impressed me so much. Forgiveness is such an ennobling thing. I felt that in the attitude of this person, I was getting a glimpse into the divine. I was getting a tiny insight into what God himself is like. I was certainly getting an insight into the teachings of Jesus.

Back to School

Eccles (Sir) 24:4-7; 1 Cor 15:54-58; Lk 6:39-45

When I was a youngster in boarding school and had yet to find my feet, the President of the college knocked at the classroom door one day and called me out by name. I nearly died with the fright. Presidents didn't come for you in the middle of a class to ask you how you were getting on. This man, a strict disciplinarian, wanted me because he already knew. I braced myself as best I could for whatever was coming my way. As I looked into his ascetic face I heard him say, through the fog, that my mother was waiting for me in the parlour. 'She has come to visit you,' he said. Now it was a strict college rule that people never visited us during class. I knew that and if I had been communicating properly my mother would know it too. This situation should never have arisen. The fact that it had was definitely my fault and mine alone. 'How long can I stay?' I ventured nervously, expecting to be executed on the spot. 'You can stay as long as you like,' he said gently, 'she's your mother'. In one short sentence he had defined himself as a person. Nothing that was said about his strictness as a President would ever weigh with me again. I had seen the man behind the mask. I knew him now not just in his role, but in his nature. The first reading today had got it right when it said, 'A man's words betray what he feels' (Eccl 1:27-61). Jesus had got it right too when he said in the Gospel: 'For a man's words flow out of what fills his heart' (Lk 6:45).

Have you and I a President's heart? What's the thrust of our feeling towards other people? What's the prevailing character of our comment? Do we use words to destroy or create? I think if we are honest with ourselves, much of what we say about other people, especially behind their backs, is negative and destructive. For some reason, best known to God, once a back is turned to us, the temptation is not to pat it but to stab! It's a sad admission to have to make but many of us are back-stabbers at heart. Inevitably, in our daily lives we are going to be talking about people. The day we stop talking about people is the day we'll all be dead. Being positive or charitable in what we say doesn't mean that we suspend our critical faculties. If others do wrong or make mistakes or get under our skin we are entitled to have our views about them. After all, a world without criticism or the making of moral judgements is a world where evil would thrive. There is, however, a clear distinction between valid criticism and malevolent comment. The malevolence has its origins not in moral concern but in envy or begrudgery or spite. Part of the reason for our malevolence is that we are happiest in life with the ineffectual. They can be the objects of our sympathy and condescension. 'Ah, the poor ould devil,' we say, 'sure there's no harm in him at all – you'd have to be sorry for him.' But the self-sufficient or successful don't enlist our sympathy at all, because we see them as a threat or as a reproach to ourselves; we make them the objects of our resentment or derision. Our deepest instinct is to pull them down. By making little of them or by robbing them of their reputation perhaps, our words have the double effect of doing them an injustice and diminishing ourselves.

There is a friend of mine who suffered a bad stroke within the past year. Its worst effect was to reduce him to silence. To be paralysed as he is, is bad enough. To be left wordless for the rest of his life is almost beyond endurance. Nothing underlines his helplessness as eloquently as does the silence. We take the gift of speech so much for granted. We fail to appreciate the degree to which words empower us and enable us to empower others. To be able to speak at all is such a wonderful privilege in itself that one of our great ambitions in life should be to encourage and affirm people rather than condemn them. And part of that encouragement and affirmation involves showing our concern for people especially at critical times in their lives. All of us have been sustained in life by the worded concern of others. Just recall for a moment how much the concerned word meant to yourself when you were sick or bereaved or alone. Those are the kind of words that make all the difference and give us the heart to go on. You open the envelope or lift the phone and a dead day comes to life. The world around you is no longer remote because a word has brought it closer. And the use of the word in a thoughtful and positive way is not just about encouraging individuals. It has a community dimension as well. Kind words don't disappear into thin air. They make for strong bonds. They are of their nature cohesive. They bring people together in friendship and mutual support. They go a long way towards the prevention or elimination of division and animosity. If stones can build high walls then the words we use can knock them. If the good word has so many beneficial effects, why on earth should we keep it to ourselves?

In his commentary on today's Gospel, a man called William Barclay makes the point that 'nothing shows the state of a man's heart so well as the words he speaks when he is saying the first thing that comes into his head'.[1] If you ask directions to a certain place for instance, one person may tell you it is near a church, another near a football ground, another still near a public house. The words used or the places identified in answer to a chance question often show where 'the interests of the heart lie'. That reminds us again of what Jesus said: 'For a man's words flow out of what fills his heart' (Lk 6:45). Words don't pour out of us of their own accord. They are dictated by the heart. If the words we use are destructive rather than creative, what we need first and foremost is not a change of vocabulary but a change of heart. In that sense and for that reason, all of us need to go back to school!

Note

1. William Barclay, *The Gospel of Luke*, Louisville, KY: Westminster John Knox Press, 2001, p. 82.

A Man of Faith

1 Kings 8:41-43; Gal 1:1-2, 6-10; Lk 7:1-10

If you were a centurion in Our Lord's time you'd have a hundred soldiers under your command. You'd probably have worked your way up through the ranks and in order to do that and keep a hundred soldiers under control you'd need to be a fairly tough guy. It wouldn't surprise anybody if you were a rough guy as well, coarse of tongue, arrogant of manner, dictatorial in style. You'd be the last person in the world that anybody would expect to carve a niche for yourself in the Gospel story or to put memorable words in the mouths of millions of Christians all over the world. 'Lord, I am not worthy to have you under my roof' (Lk 1:7). We know nothing, or at least I know nothing about any territory this nameless centurion may have conquered for his overlords in the course of his military career. What I do know is that in one brief exchange with Jesus, he conquered more hearts than any soldier in the Roman army before or since.

How come? What was it about this man that enabled him to make such an impact? Well – the first thing about him is that he wasn't your stereotypical centurion at all. He wasn't the kind of soldier we might have imagined him to be. First of all, although he was a Gentile himself, probably a Syrian, he was on excellent terms with the local Jewish population. 'He is friendly towards our people,' the Jewish elders said to Jesus (Lk 7:5), so well disposed towards them and so friendly in fact that 'he was the one who built the synagogue' (Lk 7:5). A builder of bridges too obviously! Apart from being friendly with the Jews, he was on very good terms with his own servant or slave who is described in the Gospel as 'a favourite of his' (Lk 7:2) and he was doing everything in his

THESE MIGHT HELP TOO

power to have him cured of his illness. What is perhaps most revealing of all is the gentle way he deferred to Jesus. No snapping of fingers or barking of orders here. No hint of the jackboot at all. He didn't want Jesus to put himself to the slightest trouble. He didn't want to cause him any embarrassment – much less make himself 'legally unclean' by entering a Gentile house. This Roman centurion was extraordinarily sensitive and discerning in his attitude to Jesus. He himself was the suppliant and Jesus was in command. A battle-hardened soldier he may have been, resolute and even ruthless in the pursuit of military objectives, but in his attitude to the Jewish people, to his own servant and to Jesus himself, he was a gentleman to the core!

Is that why he has carved this niche for himself in the Gospel story? Is that why his words come to daily life in the mouths of millions of Christians? Could it be that the message we are meant to carry home is that the centurion was a gent? Well, it's part of the message, but a very minor part. The heart of the message is that, above everything else, the centurion was a man of faith. He really believed that Jesus could cure his servant. Not only could he cure him, but he could cure him at a distance. His word (like the centurion's own) would be an authoritative word. It would carry weight, not just in his house, but also up in heaven. This man Jesus was from God. He had legions behind him more powerful than the Roman legions. Already somewhere in his being, the centurion could hear them marshalling in support. This man's faith was so vibrant and so pressing that it is one of the few occasions in the Gospel where Jesus confessed to being 'astonished' (Lk 7:9). Surprised, delighted, amazed, yes – but on this occasion 'astonished'. Turning around he said to the crowd, 'I tell you, not even in Israel have I found faith like this' (Lk 7:10). The centurion had made another conquest – this time in the heart of Jesus.

Speaking for myself, I find today's story particularly beautiful. There is so much tenderness in the telling of it and it has so many comforting features. The compassion of Jesus of course, the power of his word, the immediacy of his response, his inclusion of a Gentile and by implication the Gentile world in his saving ministry. Then you have the faith of the centurion, the delicacy of his approach, the depth of his humility, the relief felt by himself and his household when his servant was cured. So powerful is this story that the compassion of Jesus, the faith of the centurion and belief in their continuing interaction survive to this day the scepticism of unbelievers and our own recurring doubts. I mention our own recurring doubts because not all the centurions have their specific requests granted, in our experience. Not all our servants are cured. If Christ's word is travelling, it is not always in our direction I'm afraid. The prayers, even of the faith-filled, seem to fall so often on deaf ears. And yet overall, today's story speaks to me of universality. It suggests to us all, I think, that Jesus is the great healer over this life and the next and that the best response we can possibly make is to pray for a centurion's faith!

The Compassionate Jesus

1 Kings 17:17-24; Gal 1:11-19; Lk 7:11-17

The widow who made the biggest impression on me as a child never once struck me as being vulnerable. That was due, I think, to my lack of insight and her strength of character. Although she was in no way threatening, even in her old age, hers was a formidable presence. I can see her in my mind's eye, standing at her front door, calmly surveying the streets, giving off a distinct air of containment and self-sufficiency. She was completely in control. Although she used a stick in her declining years, she managed to give the impression that she was supporting it rather than it supporting her. Every inch of her matched it for erectness. Although she lived alone, it never occurred to me that she might be lonely. Big people weren't lonely anyway – especially big people who could hold themselves together. This woman could hold herself together as well as anyone I knew. She could do it so well in fact that I never once reflected on her condition as a widow.

I realise now of course that, like most people who live alone, she must have been very lonely indeed. As well as the loneliness of solitude, for her there was the loneliness of loss. Although relatives might pop in now and then to see that she was alright, none of them could fill the vacuum left by the death of her husband. Their life together had been sundered. She had been left on her own. The intimacy and companionship she had known was gone forever. Because she lived alone with no one to care for, most of her days would be long days. The summer evenings would be the longest of all because there would be no one to share them with and she'd find herself wondering at seven or eight o'clock if it was late enough to go to bed. There would be comfort in closing the curtains on yet another day – bringing the drag in it to an end. And there would be comfort in the voices on the radio too because they'd be directed at her as much as anybody else. She'd be part of the wider world for a while anyway. And then the bit of the day's paper she had saved up and the prayers she had still to say would bring her nearer to a night's sleep. It wouldn't have been a terrible day. The great thing about it is that it would have been tolerable.

I'd say the widow in today's Gospel had very few tolerable days since the death of her husband. Apart from the loneliness she was bound to have experienced, she had become the victim of poverty as well. Whatever about closing the curtains on the loneliness of the day, she certainly couldn't close them on the reality of destitution. Because the men were the breadwinners in biblical times, once a husband died, the widow became destitute. Her livelihood died with him. With his death, she lost the one person on whom she depended for support. As well as all that, there were no widows' pensions in her time in Palestine, no state subventions to help secure her future. The early Christians fully realised how dependent and vulnerable the widows amongst them were. 'Pure, unspoilt religion in the eyes of God our Father is this,' wrote St James. 'Coming to the help of orphans and widows when they need it and keeping oneself uncontaminated by the world' (Jas 1:27). The twelve apostles realised how dependent widows were too, especially perhaps after the Hellenists complained that the widows in their community weren't getting their fair share of the food. The apostles got seven deacons appointed to see that they did. They themselves would do the preaching. One might say then that two major concerns of the early Church were the Word and the widow (Acts 6:1-6).

There are several lessons for all of us in today's readings. First of all, the raising of the widow's son in the

Gospel is in many ways a mirror image of the miracle recorded in the first reading, so that what Luke is saying to us is that Jesus was as great a prophet as ever Elijah was. What Elijah could do, Jesus could do as well. Secondly, he is saying that there is someone here who is even greater than Elijah, because the miracle Jesus performed came 'easier' to him than the earlier one did to Elijah. One came with ease, the other only with exertion. One came on request from God, the other on instruction from Jesus. All Jesus had to say was 'rise' and at his command the young man was risen (Lk 7:15). In recognition of that authority and in the light of his subsequent resurrection, Luke has no hesitation in referring to Jesus as 'the Lord'. 'When the Lord saw her,' he says, 'he felt sorry for her' (Lk 7:13). It is the 'sorry' part, the sympathy he felt for her, that most appeals to me. Nobody cared more about the plight of this widow than Jesus did. The concern for widows shown by the early Church was in response, not just to their need, but to his example. Normally in the Gospel Jesus would perform a miracle of healing in response to a request or in recognition of faith. This was the case last Sunday in the story about the centurion. Nobody had to ask him to intervene today. Nobody had to profess faith in him either. He acted straight away, of his own accord and out of his own compassion. It was as soon as he saw her that he felt sorry for her. It was enough that she had buried her husband. It was unthinkable that she should have to bury her son – and her only son at that. Jesus felt that anyway. And what he felt in this instance was nearly as important as what he did. He knew he was giving life to two people in this situation. In raising the son from the dead, he was raising the mother from dereliction. 'Do not cry,' he said to her (Lk 7:13), realising full well, I'd say, that he was the only one there who would be able to stop her. Stop her he did. And it falls to us now, in this generation, to try to do the same. There are all sorts of people in our world, including the apparently self-sufficient, who need more than a stick to support them. Could it be that when we stand at our front door in order to survey the streets, we never notice those people at all?

On Being Thankful

2 Sam 12:7-10, 13; Gal 2:16, 19-21; Lk 7:36-8:3

Nearly every Sunday when we listen to the Gospel we find ourselves listening to a parable. Jesus was a genius at the parable but he didn't invent it. It was a literary device that was very widely used in the Mediterranean world. It was used by teachers, politicians, orators, rabbis, the lot. Among the most famous people to use the parable were Socrates and Aristotle.

Now, a parable is a story, but not every story is a parable. A parable is a particular kind of story. It has a number of distinctive characteristics. First of all, it is drawn from ordinary, everyday life. Secondly, it teaches a religious or moral lesson. Thirdly, it is intended to persuade the listener and move him or her to action.[1]

There is a parable tucked away in today's Gospel that could easily escape our attention. If that were to happen it would be a great pity because it is key to the passage as a whole. In what is known as the parable of the two debtors, the man who is owed the money, the creditor, cancels a sum of five hundred denarii for one debtor and a sum of only fifty for the other. Which of the two debtors, asks Jesus of Simon, would feel the greater gratitude? The one with the greater debt, Simon ventured cautiously. He had got it right, and apart from the invitation to Jesus to dine at his table, it was about the only thing he did get right on this particular occasion.

The two debtors in today's Gospel are the woman with the bad name and Simon the Pharisee. The woman fully realised that she had been forgiven the equivalent of five hundred denarii, whereas it would have astonished Simon that he should need the equivalent of fifty. Here then, we have the contrast between a woman who was deeply contrite and a man who was arrogantly complacent. One needed God, and the other needed a kick in the behind. Without such encouragement from the rear, Simon would never be conscious of his complacency at all. What he would be conscious of was his superiority. His primary concern in life was with sanitation. The world he inhabited was divided into two types of people – the clean and the unclean. He and his like-minded friends belonged to the cleaner section of society. The woman with the bad name and people of her ilk belonged emphatically to the other. It was unpardonable that Jesus would let such a woman touch him or that he would have anything to do with people of her variety. Already on several occasions, the Pharisees in the community, amongst whom he was proud to be numbered, had in the discharge of their moral duty and out of concern for the public good, expressed their deep unease about the behaviour of Jesus in this regard. When Levi was throwing a party, for instance, for himself and his fellow tax collectors and when Jesus and his disciples were there in the thick of it, the Pharisees had posed a crucial question by way of protest. 'Why do you eat and drink with tax collectors and sinners?' (Lk 5:30). Jesus had given them the answer that Simon must have forgotten, but that the woman with the bad name in her experience of it would never forget. 'It is not those who are well who need the doctor,' he said, 'but the sick. I have not come to call the virtuous, but sinners to repentance' (Lk 5:31-33). Here was one call to repentance that was answered with a vengeance. The woman with the bad name who had been called upon so often for the satisfaction of others now found herself called upon for her own sake and for her own salvation. Never before had she been called upon with such love. Apart from Mary's 'Magnificat', nowhere in the Gospel do we see a response so full of gratitude. Words alone could never do justice to that gratitude. The ointment she brought to anoint her saviour's feet might give some hint of it and the tears that came unbidden might do the rest. In this beautiful scene between Jesus and the woman, we get a momentary glimpse of human deliverance from the hopelessness of sin and the disdain of the self-righteous! There is permanence in the scene as well – even a touch of the eternal. Like David in the first reading, the woman's sin was forgiven; she was not to die (2 Sam 12:13). Or as Jesus himself assured her in the Gospel, her faith had saved her; she was to 'go in peace' (Lk 7:50).

Let's go back to where we began with the nature of the parable. It has three characteristics. It is taken from everyday life. It teaches a religious lesson. It wants to move us to action. That the story of creditors and debtors is from everyday life is plain to see. The lesson we are meant to take away is the need for a repentance that is full of thankfulness. The danger is that the parable we have heard and the repentance we have seen wouldn't move us to action. Are we as complacent about our sins as Simon was? Is the forgiveness we need the equivalent of no more than fifty? Is that what we think? The woman in the Gospel might have had a bad name but she gives us a great example! She had a love of Jesus – a personal devotion to Jesus – that has begun to dry up in our time! Will we keep all the ointment for ourselves? Or will we acknowledge our indebtedness to Jesus and be as grateful to him as we should? Let's think about it – and pray about it – and in time, with God's help, a few tears may come!

Note
1.   See Madeline I. Boucher, *The Parables*, Michael Glazien, 1980.

The Lamb of our Deliverance

Zech 12:10-11, 13:1; Gal 3:26-29; Lk 9:18-24

Do you know something? Most of us here have gone through an extraordinary revolution in our lifetime. I was just thinking to myself a few days ago that most of the children in this parish have never seen potatoes being dug. They've seen them in plastic bags, or in their jackets, or in the microwave, but they have never seen them being born, so to speak. They have never seen the soil breaking round them. When I look back to my own childhood, one of the expectancies of the year was the digging of the first few stalks to see what the new potatoes were like. They'd lie there, baby pink against the black soil, some of them still clinging to the root of the stalk, big ones and poitheens alike, and we'd scoop them up and bucket them and really look forward to the first taste of the new crop.

We'd give none of them to God. The Jews would! As far as they were concerned, every crop was a gift from God. So in recognition of that, as an act of thanksgiving and dependence, God would get the first spuds. They felt that the first fruits of any crop belonged especially to him. They'd offer him the first of the grain, they'd pour out the first of the wine for him, they'd even offer him a newborn lamb, killing it as a sacrifice. Then sensibly enough they'd eat it themselves and smear the blood of the lamb on the doorway of their tent or their house to show they had performed the ceremony and recognised their God. That was their spring festival and they celebrated it every year.

Then one spring, when the Jews were in slavery in Egypt, something happened that they would never forget. It's part of their history to this day. They were delivered from their slavery and led by the prophet Moses to the Promised Land.

THESE MIGHT HELP TOO

What was very significant from their point of view was that they were delivered from bondage while they were offering the first fruits to God – more especially while they were offering the lamb. They had put the blood on the doorposts. The pagan Egyptians had not. A plague or epidemic was raging. Who were hardest hit? The Egyptians! Who were spared? They were. In the confusion of the plague and the catastrophe that hit the Egyptians, the Jews escaped. After that the lamb became for them not just the lamb of first fruits but the lamb of deliverance. Not just the one they offered up but the one by which they were freed. They were saved by the blood of the lamb. And ever afterwards their spring feast was a Passover feast which celebrated their passover from being slaves to being free!

Do you remember how John the Baptist introduced Jesus to the world? He said, 'Look, there is the lamb of God, that takes away the sin of the world' (Jn 1:29). You know now why he used the word 'lamb'. He used it because Jesus would be the lamb of deliverance for us, the one who would save people by his blood, who by offering himself on the cross would deliver mankind from a slavery greater than that of Egypt – the slavery of sin and death. What's being emphasised in today's readings is the price he would pay for that deliverance. All the suffering it would cost. Zechariah in the first reading tries to convey all that by using the word 'pierced'. 'They will look on the one whom they have pierced' (Zech 12:10). The word is well-chosen, because pierced he was – pierced by the thorns, pierced by the taunts, pierced by the suffering of his mother and the disciples, pierced by the nails, pierced by our sins. In the more affluent countries like our own, in what we might describe as anaesthetised societies, where a variety of drugs help to keep pain largely under control, we are not as conscious as we might be of the degree to which our Lord suffered. Lest we forget, Luke has Jesus calling it to our attention in today's Gospel. 'The son of man is destined to suffer grievously,' he said, 'to be rejected by the elders, the chief priests and scribes and to be put to death, and to be raised up on the third day' (Lk 9:22). The Resurrection would take the sting out of his death and ours. It wouldn't take the sting out of his suffering. 'The lamb who was led to the slaughter' felt every bit of the pain (Is 5:3-7). If he calls on us in today's Gospel, as he does, 'to renounce ourselves and take up the cross' (Lk 9:23), he does so with enormous credibility, because that is precisely what he did himself.

Today then is a day to look again at the cross, to be grateful to Jesus, to feel sorry for our sins, to be resolved to overcome them. Make sure the crucifix is given an honoured place in your home and that you share the mystery and wonder of its love with your children. And let's start looking at it again ourselves with a deeper awareness of its history. Is there any other object you can think of that better demonstrates how much we matter to our Maker and how deeply, even desperately, each one of us is loved? And won't we offer to God, in return for his love, not just the first fruits, but all of the crop we can gather, the harvest of a life well lived?

Taking the Road for Jerusalem

1 Kings 19:16, 19-21; Gal 5:1, 13-18; Lk 9:51-62

I made my first visit to Lough Derg when I was about eleven or twelve. The old man with whom I travelled was doing the pilgrimage for the forty-second year in a row! Judging by its appearance and the noises it was making, so was his car! It was a Model-T Ford which served as a hen house when it wasn't on the move and which was only taken out, in a highly decorative condition, once a year for the pilgrimage to Lough Derg. The decorative material which the hens provided on a generous scale was greatly valued by the car's owner as a good luck token, though to be fair to him he brought holy water along as well, just in case! In the event, both substances worked wonders because he drove all the way to Pettigo on the wrong side of the road without hitting a thing. The time spent on the island was less stressful than the risks we took getting there, but Lough Derg still remains in my mind a very demanding pilgrimage. I remember especially the peppered water that passed for soup and tasted like penance, the cold that crept in low over the water and invaded the bones, the eyes that had an all-night, heavy-lidded battle with insistent sleep. The pilgrimage didn't last too long, however. Once you left the island it was over. We even waited up until midnight the day we went home for a compensating plateful of eggs, rashers and fried bread. What we had experienced was a temporary dip into the penitential. Although the consequences must have been beneficial and might well have been long lasting, we hadn't been on pilgrimage for life.

I mention all this because in today's Gospel Jesus set out on a pilgrimage too. His pilgrimage would take him to Jerusalem on a penitential journey that no Lough Derg pilgrim would ever undertake, or could ever envisage, in that it would result for Jesus in his passion and crucifixion. Whereas for me, my trip to the island was my first, for Jesus the journey to the city would be his last. Whereas my friend and myself would be returning after a few days to our earthly homes, Jesus was setting out on a journey that would lead him out of history into heaven. He was on his way not merely to a place but to a person, not just to a city but to ascension. That's why the Gospel says that the time was drawing near for him 'to be taken up to Heaven' (Lk 9:51). According to Luke, Jesus knew only too well what the final stage of his journey was going to cost. That's why he 'resolutely took the road' (Lk 9:51) or set his face for Jerusalem so that he might fulfil his Father's will and his own mission. He was set on a course from which he would not be deflected. There would be no turning back.

This notion of 'setting a course' or 'setting your face' or 'not turning back' is there in the first reading where Elisha follows Elijah (1 Kings 19:21) and it is very much there in the rest of today's Gospel. When the first man they met along the road said, 'I will follow you wherever you go' (Lk 9:57), Jesus was quick to remind him that he'd be leaving his home behind him and that there was no prospect of another down the road. What he'd inhabit from now on was his mission! The second and third men they met, whom Jesus called, both had something to do first, before they'd follow him. One wanted to wait and bury his father, he said; the other only wanted to bid his people goodbye. Any reasonable person, you'd imagine, would expect them, indeed encourage them, to do these things. Wouldn't we want to do them ourselves in a similar situation? The fact that Jesus seemed to be dismissive of their natural attachments and their family responsibilities is not easy to understand or defend. Perhaps they were only dithering and that he was well aware of this, or perhaps what he said to them is not meant to be taken literally. What is meant to be

THESE MIGHT HELP TOO

taken literally and very seriously indeed is that what Jesus wanted from his disciples was wholehearted commitment. The one thing that had to take priority in their lives was the preaching of the Gospel. What they were being called upon to undertake wasn't just a dip into the penitential. If there was to be no turning back for Jesus, then there could be no turning back for them. Unlike my friend and myself and our pilgrimage to Lough Derg, they'd have to be on pilgrimage for life.

Would we have followed Jesus if we had met him on the way to Jerusalem? Would you have followed him? Or would I? If we did follow him we'd be stepping out of a familiar world and embracing something new! We'd be trailblazers – and even though there's risk in that, there's tremendous excitement in it as well. It appeals to the younger side of us, the more adventurous side. The trouble is that the decision to be Christian was made for us initially by our parents. We were born into the conventional. And to a certain extent we went along with the way things were done. We'll have made personal decisions at different times along the way to do our best to follow Jesus. At confirmation, for instance. Or when we were getting married or becoming a priest or religious or whatever. And all of us will have made progress in different ways. We all have our victories. But apathy is patient, you know. And sin is even more so. They bide their time and they pull us back. They reclaim us. They are great at that kind of reclamation. And they are as happy as Larry when we've lost our enthusiasm or idealism and settled complacently into the rut that they have helped to make. Are we in a rut now? And anything but wholehearted? If we are, Jesus is asking us today for just another effort – for a greater degree of commitment. He is asking for the kind of personal devotion to himself that propelled one man so often to Lough Derg and so many, over the centuries, to Jerusalem.

Membership of Christ's Kingdom

Is 66:10-14; Gal 6:14-18; Lk 10:1-12, 17-20

There is a story told about a certain Archbishop (now deceased) who was presiding at a solemn ceremony in his cathedral. Most, if not all, of the diocesan clergy were there singing in Latin, with great gusto, as was the practice at the time. One of their number, who could always be heard but who couldn't sing at all, was giving one of his better performances. His discordant voice was audible all over and the Archbishop, a musical man himself and sensitive to such discordancy, was rapidly going mad. Having discovered that glaring down at the offending vocalist had no audible effect, he sent a priest to where the noises were coming from with a message that was urgent and to the point. 'Tell him to shut up,' he said. When the messenger reached the songbird's side and was leaning down to convey the Archbishop's good wishes, the discordant one stopped the clamour for a moment and asked curiously, 'What did he say?' 'He told you to rise it,' said the messenger, whereupon the recipient of this archiepiscopal encouragement rose to even greater heights, much to the further exasperation of the Archbishop and the amusement of those in the know.

We are told in today's Gospel that Jesus appointed seventy-two of his disciples and that he sent them on ahead of him, in pairs, to all the towns and villages that he himself was to visit (Lk 10-11). He was on the way to Jerusalem, which as we saw last Sunday was really the journey to his crucifixion, resurrection and ascension. He was on his way out of history into heaven. Because this was his final journey, it was especially important that the message he was proclaiming would be heard along the way. That's why he

THESE MIGHT HELP TOO

sent an advance party, to stir up interest, to create a sense of expectancy, to prepare the ground for what he had to say. Did you notice in the Gospel what the message was? No more than the Archbishop's, it was urgent and to the point. Unlike the Archbishop's, it wasn't telling anyone to shut up. It was, however, telling people that they'd need to change their tune. It was a message that couldn't afford to be reversed for any reason, mischievous or otherwise. It was much too serious for that. The people for whom it was intended had never heard anything like it before and would never hear anything like it again. Do you recall now what it was? It occurred twice in today's Gospel. It said simply but sensationally, 'The Kingdom of God is very near' (Lk 10:10-12).

What kind of kingdom was Jesus talking about? Well, he wasn't talking about a territorial or political kingdom. He made that clear to James and John, when, with their mother as self-appointed agent, they came to him looking for promotion (Mt 20:21). He made it clear again to Pilate at his trial when he said, 'Mine is not a kingdom of this world' (Jn 18:36). Jesus was talking about a spiritual kingdom that would represent the reign of God in the world, as distinct from the reign of humans. It would be hidden in people's hearts but evident in their lives and would be like a mustard seed in society (Mt 13:31-33).

Why did he say, 'The Kingdom of God is very near' (Lk 10:10-12)? Surely the message he was proclaiming through the disciples he sent out was that the kingdom was very near in his own person? Surely what he was saying is that, in him and his ministry, God was breaking into our world in a new and unparalleled way? Here was the intervention – the supreme and decisive intervention – that the Jewish people had been waiting for over the centuries. It is because of this that Jesus was able to say to his disciples: 'Happy the eyes that see what you see, for I tell you that many prophets and kings wanted to see what you see and never saw it; to hear what you hear and never heard it' (Lk 10:23-24).

What are the characteristics of this kingdom that Jesus brought into being? Compassion is one. Justice is another. Inclusiveness is a third. Forgiveness is a fourth. We know them well from listening to Jesus and watching him in action. We have heard him, over and over again, enunciating his values in the Sermon on the Mount and we've seen him put them into practice in a life that was caring and courageous and sacrificial. Christ is the kingdom in the way he preached and lived. He is supremely the kingdom in the way he succumbed to death and then conquered it. Christ is the kingdom in that he is love let loose in our world – love made flesh and on fire! As baptised disciples of his, we are meant to follow in his footsteps. According to Mark's Gospel, at the very beginning of his ministry, Jesus went into Galilee and said: 'The time has come and the kingdom of God is close at hand – repent and believe the good news' (Mk 1:15). This means that, for us, repentance, ongoing repentance, is essential for membership of his kingdom. The most important element of our steadfastness as Christians is that we are always changing for the better. If we are low in love, low in justice, low in forgiveness, low in prayer, low in any aspect of the Christian life, the message that's coming to us today is 'Rise it'!

The Good Samaritan

Deut 30:10-14; Col 1:15-20; Lk 10:25-37

It's very difficult to say anything new about the story of the good Samaritan. We have been down the road from Jerusalem to Jericho so many times before. We know there was a man in the ditch, and that if he was depending on the priest and the levite he'd be there yet. The good Samaritan, like the decent man that he was, took him in hand, hoisted him on his donkey, put him up at the inn, paid his expenses, with more to come perhaps, and then went on his neighbourly way. The moral of the story is clear. If you are ever in the ditch yourself and you only have the energy left for one shout, don't waste it on the first two. Save it, like a sensible man, for the good Samaritan. The other two are Gospel deaf.

Is there more to the story than that? There is! At the time that Jesus told it, it was meant to be inclusive. It was meant to broaden the understanding of neighbour and widen the embrace of love. The lawyer who pressed Jesus in today's Gospel for a precise definition of neighbour expected people other than Jews to be excluded. His neighbours were his Jewish neighbours. But who among them was he obliged to love? Who among them would be worthy of his benevolence? Would they have to be law-abiding, religious, respectable people? The answer he got from Jesus is that all anybody had to be was in some kind of need. That made him a neighbour. The definition of neighbour started with the other person's predicament and had nothing to do with his standing. What made the poor man in the story everybody's neighbour was that, in this particular situation, he had no standing at all, but happened to be lying in the ditch. The priest and the levite didn't know, presumably, whether he was one of their own or not. Not knowing, they didn't want to know. They put distance, not only between themselves and himself, but between themselves and the commandment of love as they passed indifferently by. They left a man behind them in the ditch and the bible behind them in the synagogue! They travelled light!

Is there more to the story than that even? There is! Our understanding of neighbour and our practice of love are meant to include not just the needy but the enemy. What Jesus was telling his listeners and what they found hardest to swallow was that their love should embrace the Samaritans. As far as the Jewish people were concerned, the Samaritans came, not just from a different province, but a different religion, a different lineage, almost a different planet. Whereas they confined holy scripture, for instance, to the first five books of the Bible, the Pentateuch, the Jewish people did not. Whereas they had their temple in a place called Mount Gerizim and regarded it as 'the navel of the earth', the Jews had their temple in Jerusalem. Both sides were doggedly at odds in belief and location. Worst of all from a Jewish point of view, the Samaritans were a mongrel race. Their pure Israelite blood had been polluted over centuries by intermarriage with foreign colonists imported from a place called 'Cutha'. Cutha was a bridge too far. And 'Cuthaens', as they now called the Samaritans, were a breed too low. There was a limit to what the Jews could tolerate. You can imagine the shock to their sensibilities then and their collective sense of outrage when a Samaritan was dangled before them as a model of brotherly love. Not only was the needy one their neighbour, but now the Samaritan was their neighbour too. Jesus was using the one story to give them a double message – a 'double whammy' so to speak. 'And who is my neighbour?' (Lk 10:29). Lawyers should keep their big mouths shut and not be stirring up trouble! Some questions should never be asked.

Trouble or no trouble, there are important questions we need to put to ourselves. Who are the needy in our world and how do we respond to them? Is there somebody in the ditch of loneliness or isolation that we don't help out at all? Somebody we know? Are their people whom we mean to contact but never do? People we won't visit when they are alive perhaps but whom we'll bury when they're dead? Have to make it for the funeral! Or were there people in the developing world whose funerals we might have delayed? Not because we didn't help them out now but because all we gave them was the small change? Or is there an ' enemy' in our lives with whom we refuse to be reconciled? A next door enemy? Or is their prejudice in our bones that can surface against people of a different colour or race even when we are only watching television? Armchair bigotry that is very careful to be politically correct in public! In a multicultural world there is no room for racism. The good Samaritan covered an awful lot of ground between the roadway and the ditch. He crossed the boundaries of race and religion to help a wounded man. We have ground to cover too. And boundaries to cross. One thing is for sure: cross them we never will, if we travel in the footsteps of the priest and levite and leave our bibles in the church.

Martha and Mary

Gen 18:1-10; Col 1:24-28; Lk 10:38-42

I've never been all that comfortable with today's Gospel. I've never been comfortable with the seemingly unfair comparison between Mary and Martha, with all the credit that's given to Mary for just sitting there, and the implicit criticism of Martha for not doing the same. Sure nothing would ever get done if the two of them sat down. One sitter is enough in any family.

I'm uncomfortable with it too, because all the women I've known since I was a child seemed to be Marthas. They were the kindling in our lives. They were humanity only a spoon away. There was Auntie Bea in Puntabeg for instance, about two miles outside our town. Every time we went to visit her, usually on foot, hospitality took hold of us at the door. It led us almost directly to the table, to her freshly baked bread, her tea with real milk in it, to the egg that, with its cap off, had the free range colour. Bea's table was the Lord's table. She dressed it every time for the liturgy of hospitality. That's what I remember about her and will carry to my grave. She was hospitality itself. She had it in her heart of course but she put it together with her hands.

I'd say I'm not the only one uncomfortable with today's Gospel. The first reading, for instance, speaks for itself and it cannot be all that comfortable either. If Martha was buzzing around too much within the confines of her kitchen, what are we to make of Abraham? I mean, Abraham is hospitality wound up. He has to hold the record in the bible for table-service at speed! He is described as 'running from his tent', 'hastening to find his wife', 'running to the cattle', covering more ground as a host than any host before or since (Gen 18:2-7). And apart from running round

THESE MIGHT HELP TOO

himself, he has the others on the run as well – his wife, his servants and the unfortunate calf, presumably, who was about to be caught and killed. This is what you can only describe as hectic hospitality. It is true – there is a moment of calm in the scene, when 'taking cream, milk and the calf he had prepared' he laid them before his three visitors (Gen 18:8). Calm there may have been – but there was no rest. He didn't even sit down while his visitors were eating. He wasn't a sitter at all. We're told that he remained there 'standing near them under the tree' (Gen 18:8). And to be fair to him, despite all the racing round, he did it in the same spirit as Martha did. He did it for the Lord.

What is Luke telling us in today's story? Well, for a start he's not telling us that it's better to sit than to serve. Jesus made it clear to his disciples, several times, that if they wanted to be followers of his, they would have to be servants to others. 'Anyone who would be great among you must be your servant' (Mt 20:27). By that definition, Martha had to be among the greats. She was among the fussers too, and that was her problem. Apparently, she didn't just make a meal for Our Lord; she made a meal of everything. The Gospel says she was 'distracted with all the serving ...' and 'worried and fretted' about other things as well (Lk 10:40-42). When she complained to Jesus about Mary and about all she was left to do on her own – implying at the same time that what Mary was doing was unimportant – it provided the opening for a gentle reminder. What Mary was doing was very important. She was talking and listening to Jesus. She was giving him her personal attention. For that conversation between them, however long it lasted, he was the primary person in her life. She was getting to know him better and learning from him and falling more deeply under his spell. I have to doubt that she would get the tea for him too – but all in good time.

Sometimes when I have a visitor myself, the first place I head for is the kitchen. 'You'll have a cup of tea or a coffee?'

I say – and I'm gone. And very often the visitor will say, 'Don't mind the tea or the coffee – sit down here and talk to me'. Jesus is saying the same thing. He wants every follower to be a friend. He wants us to talk to him in prayer, to listen to his word, to set aside some time for him so that he's not just a name but an intimate. He always took time out himself to commune with his father. We are told in the Gospel that, 'His reputation continued to grow, and large crowds would gather to hear him and to have their sickness cured, but he would always go off to someplace where he could be alone and pray' (Lk 5:15-16). In the early Church the apostles followed his example. They appointed deacons to feed the hungry so that they could 'devote themselves to prayer and the service of the word' (Acts 6:4). So today's Gospel is about priorities, having a balanced Christian life and making sure that Christ is central to it. It's about having a prayerful interior life as well as external activity. In other words, every Martha needs to be a bit of a Mary and every Mary a bit of a Martha. What both need to have in common – and what all of us need to have in common – is attachment to the Lord.

Confidence in God

Gen 18:20-32; Col 2:12-14; Lk 11:1-13

'You can stay at home from school tomorrow,' my father would say now and again, 'and you can foot some more of that turf out there in the bog.' Footing turf, as some of you will know, was standing four or five sods at a slant, with one or two on top, the better to dry them out. It was tedious, back-breaking work, but it was better than making mathematical problems or sums stand up in school! So as soon as the bog was mentioned I'd start to pray. The only thing you couldn't depend on was the weather. The following morning almost without fail, the rain would be coming down in buckets. The clouds would be leaning down, in black heaps, over the roofs of the houses. I'd be in and out to the front door, growing more and more despondent, to see if there was any lift in the sky. I thought I could see a lift sometimes. My mother couldn't. My father couldn't. And God wouldn't. Why did he say 'ask and it will be given to you' in the first place (Lk 11:9)? Why did he say that? He had no interest in footing turf at all. We could all perish for the winter as far as he was concerned! I'd put another bit of scepticism into my school bag and make my way dejectedly to school.

God has made it up to me since in more ways than one. Indeed he did then, in the family into which I was born and the town in which I grew up. He has done that or similar things for all of us. He has answered prayers we never said and given us gifts for which we never asked and to which we have no entitlement. He is saying 'yes' to us, all the time, in the air we breathe, in the colours we can distinguish, in all our experiences of love. Our variety is God's gift. There is no one who gives more to us than God. If there are misers amongst us, he's not one of them. We mustn't get hung up on 'refusals'. Yet God does refuse us at times. He takes from us, despite our entreaties, the people who mean most in our lives. He leaves us the whole world and takes the one person who made the difference. The man in today's parable may get up in the middle of the night and give three loaves to the friend who keeps knocking on the door. There are doors we knock on that God doesn't open. That's our experience when it comes to specific requests. There is no use in trying to pretend otherwise. It only does a disservice to the faith.

So the question is, is it worth our while praying for particular things at all? Like healing, for instance, for ourselves or somebody else? Will the rain be coming down in buckets and the clouds heavy over the houses no matter how we pray? Does God ever respond? Well, judging by what he did, in the Gospels, in the person of Christ, he certainly does. Think of all the people he healed, because he was asked: the Centurion's servant (Mt 8:5-13); the Canaanite woman's daughter (Mt 15:21-23); the man with the withered hand (Mt 12:9-14); the blind beggar Bartimaeus, who followed him down the road (Mk 10:46-52) ... the list goes on and on! And persistence in prayer helped to lengthen it. There is a wonderful moment in the Gospels – a very revealing moment that brings God and prayer together as in a snapshot – that shows how responsive God is to prayer. It's about the leper who came to Jesus one time and 'pleaded on his knees'. 'If you want to,' he said, 'you can cure me' (Mk 1:40). We're told that Jesus felt sorry for him, that he stretched out his hand and touched him. 'Of course I want to,' he said ... 'Be cured' (Mk 1:42). It is the nature of God to reach out and touch. Does God respond to our prayer? The word from heaven is 'of course ... of course!' (Mk 1:42).

But God, as we've said, doesn't always give us what we ask for, for reasons best known to himself. Even as our hearts break and our minds run wild with grief, the silence from on high is deafening. In our experience, people who don't answer aren't there or don't want to be there. It is God's apparent indifference that fills us with so much anger at times and even makes us doubt his existence. Yet, Jesus assures us in today's Gospel that God is not only there, but there as our father (Lk 11:2). And if earthly fathers won't give their children stones when what they need is bread, our heavenly father won't give us stones either (Lk 11:11). What he will give us in answer to our prayer is the spirit we need to cope with life's difficulties (Lk 11:13). There is no escape in our world from the mistakes we make, the illness that debilitates, the accident that kills. So we must trust the Father to see us through, just as Jesus trusted him in the garden of Gethsemane. 'Let your will be done, not mine' (Lk 22:42). I remember when I was a young lad learning to swim, my father would hold his two hands under my body in the water and encourage me to make waves with my arms and kick with my legs. I could do that in the knowledge and confidence that he would hold me up – that he wouldn't let me down. When we are at our lowest in life and struggling to keep afloat, we must pray for that kind of confidence in God – two-handed confidence. If we can do that and learn to trust him, then the clouds over the houses will break all the sooner and we'll see the lift in the sky!

Making Ourselves Rich

Eccl 1:2, 2:21-23; Col 3:1-5, 9-11; Lk 12:13-21

I don't want to depress you but in the past five years over a hundred people have died in this parish. In all probability, unless there is something we don't foresee, roughly the same number will die during the five years to come. Who will be included in that number we don't know. What it does suggest to us though is that we don't live in a permanent community, but in a community that's subject to constant change, especially the enormously heart-breaking changes that are brought about by death. Time is a patient killer, by and large. It takes its time and it bides its time. But it is continually making inroads into our limited lives. Our expiring resources. And it does it very stealthily. Ezra Pound, the American poet, put it very well when he wrote: 'And the days are not full enough, And the nights are not full enough, And life slips by like a field mouse not shaking the grass.'

I'm saying all this to you because today's readings are telling us at least three things. First of all, they are reminding us that life is short, that death is poised to strike at any one of us when we least expect it. It struck at the rich man in the parable on the one night in his life that he felt most secure. He had built his barns. He had all the space he needed now. But he hadn't the time. Even as he was building his barns, the foundation beneath his own feet was giving way. Bricks and mortar would last much longer in his case than flesh and blood. He was building a monument to his own mortality. He was securing his own future at a time when his future was gone. There was irony in his building and in his fate. 'Vanity of vanities,' the preacher said, 'all is vanity' (Eccl 1:2).

The second point the readings make is that, seeing life is so short, our entire focus or even our primary focus shouldn't be on the making of money. There is no life without it, we know, but there is more to life than making it. Since life is so precious in itself, it is foolish to merely mint it. What is particularly foolish is to become a hoarder. In that situation, one person's obsession becomes another person's windfall. The fruit you try to hold on to in the branches of your tree topples, when you topple, into somebody else's lap. There are no apples in the next life, as far as we know. The rich man's hoard in the Gospel went inevitably to somebody else. The money we pile up and worship is never its own reward. It's always somebody else's inheritance. The readings don't discount the benefits of inheritance to family or charity or friends. They don't discuss these things at all. The main point they make is that money shouldn't be our God.

The third thing the readings say, or the Gospel says at any rate, is not that we shouldn't make a god of money just because life is short and there are better things to be doing. What the Gospel is saying is that we shouldn't make a god of money because we have to face the real God in judgement. God said to the rich man in today's Gospel: 'Fool, this very night the demand will be made for your soul' (Lk 12:20). The rich man is called fool in the biblical sense, as one who says in his heart 'there is no God'. He is not a believer. There are barns, and bigger barns 'and plenty of good things' for years and years to come (Lk 12:19) but there is no God. His whole attitude betrays his godlessness. He prefers earthly roofs to heavenly riches. His 'thoughts won't be on the heavenly things' that Paul is recommending in the second reading. (Col 3:2). He won't have a notion of 'killing everything that belongs only to earthly life – especially greed' (Col 3:5). No, he has built his barns for his greed! He'll be gorging his way through his granaries for the rest of his life instead of 'making himself rich in the sight of God' (Lk 12:21).

May I come back in conclusion to the point I never left? We are only passing through. Time has caught up with us that little bit more since I began to talk. The field mouse is moving through the grass. What's left to us is gift! If our next project in life is the bigger barn, if our only remaining ambition is to gorge our way through our granaries to the exclusion of God and other people, then we need to take stock. We don't have to be 'foolish' in the biblical sense! Perhaps the best way to bring God into our lives again is through concern for his people. Most of those who died in the parish in the past five years were elderly. That's the nature of things. Most of those who will die in the next five years will more than likely be elderly as well. Let's keep that in mind. Let it influence the way we treat people – all people, but especially the elderly. We cannot deny time its progress in this life or its triumph. The one thing we can deny time is regret. It's a great thing to be able to say when someone we love dies, 'I'll miss him very much – but I have no regrets'. All our regrets are inside ourselves. Let's try to get outside ourselves and centre our lives on the other – on the other person and on God. Some of the richest people we meet in this life have no big barns at all.

THESE MIGHT HELP TOO

Being a Good Steward

Wis 18:6-9; Heb 11:1-2, 8-19; Lk 12:32-48

I have a photograph on the mantelpiece inside in the parish house. It's a photograph of an old man, a lifelong friend of mine, and it was taken the last time he came to visit me, shortly before he died. The expression on his face the night the photo was taken was developed over eight years in the dark room of suffering. I say that because eight years before he was the victim of a serious stroke that shackled him physically but failed to deaden his heart. There was a spirit in the man that no stroke could reach and that death itself has never quenched. He was one of those lovely human beings of whom it was a privilege to know. He had many things to do in life. He had a profession to follow, a business to run, a family to care for, a community to serve, a God to adore, a fund of stories to tell, and he did all of them remarkably well. He undertook them with a degree of seriousness and humour that was even better as a blend than as a paradox. He was human nature at its best. I'm talking about him today because Jesus is asking in the Gospel, 'what sort of steward is faithful and wise enough for the master to place him over his household?' (Lk 12:42). And I'm saying to Jesus: 'Yer man on the mantelpiece was one.'

He wasn't the only one of course. There are men and women on mantelpieces all over the place. And the faithful and wise stewards that we are talking about aren't all in the past. They are in every parish in the present, including our own. There is so much stewardship going on in this parish for instance, that we hardly notice it at all. So much of it is so obvious that it is almost invisible. Young parents walking the floor at night with babies that have wind in their tummies. Slightly older parents trying to cope with teenagers that have too much wind in their sails. Members of a family rallying round when an older member needs support. Immediate and compassionate response when a shadow shows up in an x-ray that casts a much larger shadow at home. Wise and faithful stewardship is what keeps this community together. Caring for one another. It's what enables us to face the day. The Gospel doesn't recommend the impossible. Most of the time it is celebrating the actual. Whether you are married or not, whether you are old or young, everyone of you listening to me now is exercising stewardship, to some degree at least. No one of us is starting from scratch!

There is none of us who hasn't something to learn either or who doesn't need to be challenged to a higher level of stewardship. We live as a people between two comings – the coming of Christ in the incarnation and his coming again in judgement. We are being reminded in today's Gospel to prepare for his coming: 'to store up treasure in heaven' (Lk 12:33); 'to be dressed for action, have our lamps lit, to be ready to open the door as soon as [the Master] comes and knocks' (Lk 12:35-36). The rich man in last Sunday's Gospel went in for big barns. We are being warned today not to go in for big blunders! That's what the unfaithful servant did in today's Gospel. He lost the run of himself. He ate and drank to excess. He beat the 'menservants and the maids' (Lk 12:46). He put restraint, responsibility and justice on the back burner. He ignored his God and ill-treated his people. He put himself in danger of living between two goings – of going to pot and going to hell. Jesus didn't mince his words when he was describing what was in store for him. 'The Master will cut him off,' he said, 'and send him to the same fate as the unfaithful' (Lk 12:46).

There is a word in today's readings for those of us who are going through a rough time. The expressions on more faces than one are developed in the dark room of suffering. My friend wasn't the only one to suffer! I don't know whether you noticed but there are a few references in the readings to the 'night'. In the first reading, the Jews endured a long night of slavery from which they were eventually delivered. In the second reading, Abraham went through a long night of blind faith or trust in God before reaching the Promised Land. In the Gospel, the disciples were expected to stay awake all night long if necessary for the coming of their Master. Sometimes, in the course of our lives, we experience the darkness of the night ourselves. The darkness of suffering like the Israelites, or of blind faith like Abraham, or of spiritual struggle like the disciples. When the night of doubt or despondency or grief or sin descends on us, we can easily lose heart and feel terribly alone. But please remember this. For those who persevere in faith like the Israelites, or Abraham, or the disciples, the night can be a night of deliverance. Nobody knows that better than Jesus himself who was delivered from the darkness of the cross in the dawn of resurrection. Christ is our light. He is unquenchable light! And he has one wonderful sentence in today's Gospel that I'd love you to take home with you! It says, 'There is no need to be afraid, little flock, for it has pleased your Father to give you the Kingdom' (Lk 12:32).

The Gospel of the Sword

Jer 38:4-6, 8-10; Heb 12:1-4; Lk 12:49-53

Let me begin by telling you three short stories. Very short stories! The first is about Jesus. He was preaching one day in Jerusalem and some people were so impressed that they concluded he must be 'the Christ' (Jn 7:41). Other people weren't persuaded at all. How could the Christ be from Galilee, they argued. Wasn't he supposed to come from Bethlehem? And the Gospel says, 'the people couldn't agree about him' (Jn 7:43). They were divided. The second story is about Jesus as well. About the time he put paste on a man's eyes and put an end to his blindness. He did that on the Sabbath. The Pharisees took the view that if he wouldn't keep the Sabbath he couldn't be from God. But others saw it differently! The healing of a blind man couldn't be the work of a sinner. And the Gospel says there was disagreement among them (Jn 9:16). Divided again! No marks for guessing who the third story is about. After healing the blind man, Jesus spoke at length to the Pharisees. According to St John's account of it, he would lay down his life of his own free will, he told them, and he had it in his power to take it up again (Jn 10:18). Some of his hearers were incensed. The man had to be 'possessed' to be saying things like that (Jn 10:20)! But others weren't so sure. He couldn't possibly be possessed. How could the devil be in the detail of a blind man's sight? Divided yet again!

We read about incidents like that in the Gospel every now and again but it's only when you put a few of them together that you realise how divisive a figure Jesus really was. We think of him as a unifier, as one whose role in life was to bring people together. And of course that's what he wanted to do. The promotion of peace, the practice of love,

THESE MIGHT HELP TOO

were primary concerns of his, at the top of his agenda. 'Happy are the peacemakers,' he said (Mt 5:9). 'Love one another as I have loved you' (Jn 15:12). It was his most fervent desire that the Jewish people first and the people of other nations later would accept him as the Messiah so that all could be united in his kingdom. It had to be the great sadness of his life that so many of his own people rejected him. The words he addressed to the people of Jerusalem have to be among the most poignant not just in Scripture but in all literature. 'Jerusalem, Jerusalem, you that kill the prophets and stone those who are sent to you. How often have I longed to gather your children as a hen gathers her chicks under her wings and you refused' (Mt 23:37).

But even though he was saddened by rejection, Jesus knew in his heart that in his person and in his preaching he was bound to cause division. He makes that abundantly clear in today's Gospel. Just as Jeremiah had met with opposition in his time (as described in the first reading) so Jesus would meet opposition in his. The experience of one would prefigure the other. 'I have come to bring fire to the earth,' Jesus said, 'and how I wish it were blazing already' (Lk 12:49). What he is saying is that people would be purified and separated in the fire of his challenge. He wasn't going to be an innocuous presence in the world. People would either accept him as the Saviour or they wouldn't. They'd either be for him or against him. In that sense, he hadn't come to bring peace on earth (Lk 12:51). He had not come 'to bring peace but a sword' (Mt 10:34). The sword would bring pain as swords inevitably do. And the sword would bring parting in terms of choice and allegiance. Members of families would find themselves on opposite sides. It happened in Jesus' lifetime when members of Jewish and even Gentile families became his followers. It had happened in Luke's time as well. That is why he is talking about it in today's Gospel. Some were converted to Jesus and others were simply convulsed. Jesus would never be a blunt instrument. But his message would have a clean edge. His Gospel of peace could also be a Gospel of the sword.

Could Christ's claim give rise to division within our families nowadays? Could father and son or mother and daughter be at odds on matters of faith? They could indeed! And they sometimes are. It is one of the ironies of history that in the early Church many of the younger people would become followers of Jesus to the consternation of their Jewish parents, whereas in modern times in our own country, parental consternation is caused by a tendency among the young to walk away. Not that this tendency is confined to the young or that it represents a total abandonment of Jesus. It does not. What it does represent generally is a failure to celebrate the Eucharist regularly, a rejection of traditional Christian teaching on sexual morality, a decline in devotional life, an absence of the prayerfulness so characteristic of the older generation. It may be true as well of course that some people, young and old, love Jesus very much as the greatest of the prophets without being able to acclaim him as the Son of God. One thing we can be sure of anyway is that when children lapse in faith or lose it entirely, the pain felt by believing parents runs very deep. Is there anything to be said that might help them to cope?

Well, the first thing I'd say is that Jesus would hardly see himself as a catalyst for conflict, least of all within a family. He didn't set out deliberately to disrupt. His hope would be that we might die for him without killing one another. Divided in faith we might be in terms of adherence or non-adherence to himself. His primary injunction, however, is that all of us should be united in love. If some stop believing, no one should stop loving. The second thing I'd say is that none of us can insist on another person's faith. Faith is not a matter of insistence. In human terms it has to be for each person a matter of discovery. We come to faith, if we do,

THESE MIGHT HELP TOO

along a route where there are no footprints other than our own. No one can map our journey for us. People can give us directions alright, at the start and along the way. But the twists and turns we experience and the markings we leave behind us will be peculiarly our own. It's my journey, with God's help and your encouragement. The third thing I'd say is this. Let those of us, young and old, who wish to follow Jesus, renew today our own commitment. That's what Paul is saying to us in the second reading. He is telling us to 'keep running steadily in the race we have started'. 'Let us not lose sight of Jesus,' he says, 'who leads us in our faith and brings it to perfection' (Heb 12:2). The steadier we are and the closer we come to Jesus the more of a help we will be to others and the happier we'll be ourselves. The fire that Jesus started two thousand years ago is meant to be burning at its fiercest in our own hearts.

The Narrow Door

Is 66:18-21; Heb 12:5-7, 11-13; Lk 13:22-30

Did you get the impression from today's Gospel that very few people are saved, that salvation is at best difficult and at worst impossible? You are either in through the gap as fast as you can, while the gap is still there, or you are wasting your time knocking at a door that's closed to you forever. Heaven, as Jesus seems to describe it, is essentially impregnable. It's there to keep people out, even those who are dying to get in! That's not the way we think about heaven at all. Our heaven is of its nature accessible. We are reasonably confident that the vast majority of people who have died, including our own, are already up there. And it never occurred to us that they'd have to be shooting through gaps or pushing and shoving to get in. It never occurred to us either that Jesus would have his shoulder to the door. 'You're out – and stay out!' The only thing we ever associated with his shoulder was the cross that he carried for our sake. Which of them is the real Jesus?

The real Jesus of course is Jesus of the Cross, not the Jesus of the closed door. In order to understand today's Gospel it is very important to put it in context. The first phrase that puts it in its immediate context is in the first sentence. It tells us that Jesus was 'making his way to Jerusalem' (Lk 13:22). In other words, he was going to the place of his destiny. He was making his way to the cross. This then was his final journey, the last time he would pass through these 'towns and villages' (Lk 13:22), the last opportunity he would have to win the people to himself and offer them salvation. He had begun his public mission with an impassioned plea to people to 'repent and believe the good news' (Mk 1:15). If there was an urgency about it then,

THESE MIGHT HELP TOO

and there was, there was a greater urgency about it now. His public mission was coming to a close. The cross was looming larger, the end was drawing near – time was running out for himself and for his listeners. Jesus had come on a universal mission. Above all, he wanted more than 'a few' to be saved. When asked if only a few would be saved, he didn't answer the question directly (Lk 13:23). What he did say, and say most emphatically, was that salvation shouldn't be taken for granted. It was a 'narrow door' (Lk 13:24), an opportunity they were getting now that might never come their way again. It was a narrow door as well in that it involved the dumping of selfishness and scepticism in order to become his disciple. People not prepared to do this would never make it through the door. Among these would be the members of the Jewish religious establishment, who had refused to accept him up to that point. Jesus was very concerned about that. If they persisted in their obstinacy and in their determination to reject him, the vacuum they left behind would be filled by the Gentiles. Isaiah could foresee them coming in their thousands to the 'holy mountain in Jerusalem from all the nations' (Is 66:20). Jesus predicted it himself too. From 'east and west they would come and from north and south ... to take their places at the feast in the Kingdom of God' (Lk 13:29). 'Those now last would be first,' he said, 'and those now first would be last' (Lk 13:30). Jesus wanted everybody to be saved and he didn't want his own people to exclude themselves. So the time for decision had come. The time for choosing had come. It was a question of now or never.

Once the door had been closed on the rusted hinges of obstinacy, there would be no opening of it again. A 'yes' now was better than a knock later. If a knock later was a knock wasted, why not say 'yes' now?

And what about ourselves? Are we taking our salvation for granted – going on the presumption that no matter what way we live, we shall be saved regardless? I'm afraid the way to salvation is a little narrower than that. It calls for specifics, like faith in Jesus, our Saviour, repenting of our sins, keeping his commandments, especially his commandment of love. There is a road we are meant to travel that is tarred and clearly marked for us. If we ignore the markings and stray into the soft margins, the danger is that we will sink. Jesus is preaching in our town and village today just as he preached in the towns and villages of Galilee. He wants to add to the harvesting of the cross. He is calling on each one of us with great urgency to come with him. I know we are here. But are we spiritually here? Spiritually happy? Spiritually content? Is there a closed door in our lives, on rusted hinges, that we could be knocking on when it is too late? Today is a day for decision! A day for choosing! If a knock later on might be a knock that is wasted, why not say 'yes' now?

Humility

Eccles (Sir) 3:17-20, 28-29; Heb 12:18-19, 22-24; Lk 14:1, 7-14

No marks at all today for identifying the main theme in the readings. It is, of course, the theme of humility. 'The greater you are,' the first reading tells us, 'the more you should behave humbly' (Eccl 3:18). Then, in the Gospel, Jesus tells us that in his kingdom, symbolised by the wedding feast, we shouldn't be trying to lord it over anybody or we could end up being put in our place. 'For everyone who exalts himself will be humbled,' he says, 'and the man who humbles himself will be exalted' (Lk 14:11).

The first thought that occurs about humility is that most, if not all, of us think we have it. Pride and arrogance are vices that we attribute to somebody else. I've yet to hear somebody say, including myself, 'I'm full of my own importance'. We may admit to a little pride now and again, but that is presumed to be an aberration. We are basically humble people, we think, and are bound to be perceived that way by everybody. So humble are we in fact that we are inclined to be proud of it! Is it possible that we may have something to learn?

The second thing that occurs is that our concept of humility may be limited. We may think of it solely in terms of the kind of people we are and the way we treat others, that we shouldn't be making too much of ourselves or too little of anybody else. We think of it in terms of evenness, not getting above ourselves or losing the run of ourselves. That kind of humility is fine and highly commendable. The only trouble with it is that it is entirely earthbound. It lives under a low ceiling. It looks inwards and outwards but never upwards. It never really sees the sky.

Christian humility always sees the sky. The one person it never loses sight of is God. There was a time in our lives when we saw the wonder of God's creation in everything, when a darting trout in a stream or a hedgehog curling in a ditch left us wide-eyed with astonishment. I remember the first time I ever saw the sea. We were on the road towards Enniscrone in Co. Sligo. We were travelling around a bend in an open horse-drawn carriage – adults and children together – when the sea with an expansiveness that was never ending came suddenly into view. We jumped up in acknowledgement of it – us children, I mean – and with a kind of primeval shrillness called the world's attention to it. 'Look, look!' we shouted excitedly. 'The sea! The sea!' But the world had seen it before and was seeing it again only in our excitement. When we lose our sense of wonder, we are losing some of our humility. 'Glory be to God for dappled things', Gerard Manley Hopkins wrote in 'Pied Beauty'. And again, in 'God's Grandeur', 'The world is filled with the grandeur of God'. The more we see of God's grandeur and the more we give thanks for it, the humbler we are.

The more grateful we are for what God has done for us, the humbler we are too. Gratitude and humility go together. When we see the crib at Christmas, for instance, somebody will have set it up and somebody else will have carved the figures for it, but God will have given it its meaning. Only God could have written the script: 'God loved the world so much that he gave his only Son, so that everyone who believes in him may not be lost but may have eternal life' (Jn 3:16). When we look at the cross we know it was man who made it for death but God who remade it for life. When we look at the statue of Mary we know that here is one person who never forgot what she owed him. 'My soul proclaims the greatness of the Lord,' she said, 'and my spirit exults in God my Saviour; for the Almighty has done great things for me and holy is his name' (Lk 1:46, 49). 'Christian humility is sustained by a grateful memory of what the Lord has done for us,' wrote Bernard Haring.[1] St Augustine said much the same thing in a work called *The City of God*. 'It is an essential element of humility,' he wrote, 'that it directs the heart to what is above.'[2] Pride makes us look down; turning our back on God, looking down on others. Humility keeps us close to the ground but makes us look up!

One of the biggest reasons for humility before God is that we are all sinners! Can sinners afford to be proud? When the begrudgery of our sin is measured against the munificence of God's mercy it should make us humbler still. To think that he forgives anything and everything – if only we will repent! The best place to find the humility we are talking about is at the back of the temple in Jerusalem. That, according to Jesus, is where the publican stood when he gave classic expression to it. 'God, be merciful to me a sinner,' he said (Lk 18:14). If God has his ear cocked in heaven for one thing more than another, I'd say the publican put it into words for us, for all time!

Notes

1. Bernard Haring, *Free and Faithful in Christ*, Vol. 1, St Paul Publications, 1978, p. 203.
2. *The City of God* by St Augustine, Book 14, Ch. 13.

A Role for the Smaller Fry

Wis 9:13-18; Philem 9:10, 12-17; Lk 14:25-33

He didn't hate his own family. Jesus, I mean! We don't know an awful lot about his relationship with Joseph for instance, but the little we do know suggests that they got on very well. When Jesus got lost at twelve years of age in a Jerusalem temple that was packed for the passover, Joseph was as anxious to find him as Mary was – or similarly anxious at least. 'They were overcome when they saw him,' the Gospel tells us, 'and his mother said to him, "My child why have you done this to us? See how worried your father and I have been looking for you"' (Lk 2:48). Luke continues his account of the incident by saying, 'He then went down with them and came to Nazareth and lived under their authority' (Lk 2:51). No hint of hatred there. No suggestion that their authority was imposed on him. On the contrary, the implication is that it was lovingly accepted. No hint of hatred in Luke's final comment either. 'And Jesus increased in wisdom, in stature and in favour with God and men' (Lk 2:52).

Why then does today's Gospel require hatred of family as a condition of discipleship? Why should we have to hate our parents when Jesus didn't hate his? Did we all misunderstand the fourth commandment when it told us to 'honour our father and mother'? Even when they were warming the bottle for us as babies, were we supposed to be making faces behind their backs? 'Just you wait until I grow up.' And isn't this incitement to hatred completely at odds with our better instincts and similarly at odds with Jesus' own teaching? 'I give you a new commandment,' he said to us, 'love one another just as I have loved you. By this love you have for one another, everyone will know that you are my disciples' (Jn 13:14-15). Are the members of our own family the only enemies to be excluded from our love? Anyway, isn't Jesus himself incarnate love? How could incarnate love be the genesis of hate?

When Jesus used the word 'hate' in the Gospel in relation to family, he wasn't talking in terms of animosity, hostility or even dislike. He wasn't talking about negative feelings towards family at all. What he was talking about was consequences, the consequences of choice! If you want to be my disciple, he's saying, the demands it will make on you will be enormous. It will mean becoming a member of a spiritual family that will involve huge sacrifices for your own. It will mean more than a few 'hear-hears' from the back of the crowd. It will mean more than turning up for the odd meeting and licking a few envelopes to advance the campaign. It will mean following me to the end of the road – and maybe beyond. It will mean attaching yourself to my person, playing a full part in my mission, trudging by my side through the towns and villages of Galilee, setting your face like mine for the city of Jerusalem while retaining the residual courage to confront what may befall us there. The people who were listening to Jesus had at least an incipient understanding of what their discipleship involved. Many of those he invited to follow him were engaged in the fishing industry around the sea of Galilee. The first four whom he called – Peter, Andrew, James and John – were either casting nets or mending them. They were big into fishing, not as a hobby but as a livelihood. There is a suggestion in the Gospel of St Mark that Zebedee, the father of James and John, was running a sizeable commercial operation. Mark informs us that he had 'hired servants' (Mk 1:20). The first four were well aware therefore that they were cutting their nets adrift and leaving livelihood and home behind, for the foreseeable future anyway. They were leaving love for loneliness perhaps, security for insecurity, the skills they knew for skills they had yet to learn. They had already begun to walk upon the water, these four. In so far as human beings are capable of it, they were giving their all. Unlike the aspiring builder in today's Gospel or the belligerent king with more notions than troops, they had it in them to finish the tower as well as finish the war. They understood, in embryo at least, that discipleship involved sacrifice and commitment.

Everybody in this congregation and many who are not here at all are being called by Christ to discipleship. The mission upon which he embarked two thousand years ago and which has gained such momentum in the meantime is every bit as important now as it was then. One big difference of course is that Christ is not standing before us, looking us straight in the eye, getting our full attention and urging us with all his persuasive power to join him in an historic enterprise that would lead to the salvation of humankind. He is still calling us, though, in person and as individuals. Each one of us matters as much to him as Peter did, as Andrew or James or John. If all of them were needed then, then all of us are needed now. We'll never attain their eminence, of course, or be the foundational figures that they became. But if there was a role in Christ's Church for the bigger fish, then there has to be a continuing role for the smaller fry. May we attach ourselves to his person, care for his people, adhere to his commandments, celebrate his Eucharist, be a part, if only a broken part, of his saving mission. If he were to stand before you now, look you in the eye, and call you to be his disciple, what would you want to say to him – 'no', or 'yes'?

Note

1. Sean Freyne, *Jesus, a Jewish Galilean*, T. & T. Clark Publishers, 2004, p. 49f.

Repentance

Exod 32:7-11, 13-14; 1 Tim 1:12-17; Lk 15:1-32

When I was growing up there was a lady across the street from us who had two nephews. Both of them were priests. They would come every now and again to take a holiday with herself and her husband. One of the priests worked on the English Mission and was greatly loved by every one who knew him. The other man, a quieter type, but no less loved in our neighbourhood, was working in America in one of the southern states. His name was Fr Eddie. There was a great deal of discrimination against black people in the American southern states at the time – including discrimination by those who professed to be religious. Their God preferred separate approaches, apparently, when it came to worship or intercession. If blacks and whites were to pray together in the same church, God was bound to get terribly confused. Fr Eddie didn't agree, so he did something that hadn't been done before in the parish: he invited his black parishioners to come to mass in a parish church hitherto reserved for whites. Some of them came. Fr Eddie left. He was forced to leave. Some of his white parishioners frog-marched him out of town with a rifle in his back. They frog-marched him into my consciousness too as a hero. He retains that heroic stature in my memory but whether he ever got back to his parish again, I just don't know!

Now the frog-marchers in that incident would get on very well with the Scribes and Pharisees in today's Gospel. One thing they had in common was a deep sense of their own superiority, on racial grounds in one case, on moral grounds in the other. The Scribes and Pharisees regarded themselves as the religious elite. They were the lily-whites who, by and large, adhered to the Mosaic Law in a rigorous, self-righteous way but who would have no truck whatever with a morally off-white underclass known as the 'tax collectors and sinners'. Those who collected taxes for the Romans were never going to be popular anyway but when their exactments included a hefty percentage for themselves, they were going to be despised for their dishonesty as well. The term 'sinners' covered a great variety of people. It included robbers, adulterers, prostitutes – all kinds of sinners in fact. It even included shepherds who could not always be relied on for honesty and devotion to duty. Now Jesus sat at table with the Scribes and Pharisees – at their table and his own. But he did exactly the same with the tax collectors and sinners. He made no distinctions. He refused to discriminate. It was this aspect of his behaviour that shocked the Scribes and Pharisees to the core. As far as they were concerned, what he was doing wasn't just *infra dig* or socially distasteful, it was downright irreligious as well.

It is because Jesus wanted them to understand why he was doing what he was doing that he told the two parables in today's Gospel. If you are a shepherd and you find the sheep that you had lost, you are delighted. If you are a poor widow – and there were none poorer than in Palestine – and you find the coin that you had lost, you are delighted. If a sinner you had lost comes back to your table as a sign of repentance, you in your turn extend the warmest of welcomes as a sign of forgiveness because you are delighted as well. The table for Jesus was not just for food but for fellowship and reconciliation. These stories he tells are all about God's infinitely forgiving nature and the delight he experiences when sinners like ourselves repent. 'I tell you, there will be more rejoicing in heaven over one repentant sinner than over ninety-nine virtuous men who have no need of repentance' (Lk 15:7).

Two thoughts occur. The first is that unless Jesus was deluded, which he wasn't, there can be no doubt

THESE MIGHT HELP TOO

whatsoever about God's love for each one of us. Just as a parent loves the individual child, no matter how big the family, in the same way God loves every individual person. Some people have a great head for names. There is nobody with a better head for names than God. 'I have called you by your name, you are mine.' The second thought that occurs is that many of us may not belong to either group in today's Gospel, the Pharisees or the repentant sinners. We may belong to a group that was always there but that seems to be increasing in number: the group of the unconcerned. And there are two things we have tended to do. We have tended to redefine sin downwards and we have tended not to repent of it at all. Having emasculated one, we see no need for the other. We do what we feel like doing, whether it is moral or not. We are choosing the indulgent way and we are losing our conscience. So much public evil all round us and so little personal sin of our own! Those who were guilty of injustice or exploitation or impurity in Our Lord's time acknowledged that and repented of it. Well, some of them did anyway! That's why they gave rise to such rejoicing in heaven. Is there much rejoicing in heaven about us? Are we driving them delirious? Is there sin in our lives that we refuse to acknowledge? And when did we last repent of it in the Sacrament of Reconciliation? Are the stories in today's Gospel meant for everybody else except me?

The Use of Money

Amos 8:4-7; 1 Tim 2:1-8; Lk 16:1-13

I once spent a whole day working in a man's garden, mainly because he asked me but partly because I'd make a bit of money. I was only a young lad at the time and had no regular income, apart from what my parents or some generous adult gave me. The owner of the garden wasn't noted for throwing money around, but he was a friend of the family and he wouldn't have to part with a lot to enable a young lad to go to the pictures that night. He came out to the garden a few times as the evening wore on, made approving noises about the work that had been done but kept his hands discouragingly in his trousers pockets. As the sun was sinking in a copper-coloured sky, the only sign of copper around, I presented myself at the front door of my employer's house with reasonable if not confident expectations of some financial recompense for all I had done. 'Thank you very much,' he said – which was nice of him – 'you had better go home now to your tea because your Mammy will be expecting you.' I couldn't get over it, all the way home, how any man could be so mean!

He wasn't the only one, of course. We all know that money, which is so necessary for living, can also be a very negative force in the formation of attitude and the casting of character. I wasn't the only one to be sent home without the price of the pictures. There are stingy owners of gardens all over the place. 'They have their confirmation money,' we say, or 'they wouldn't spend the Christmas'. The sad thing is that in holding on to their money they lose their reputation. They have wealth without warmth! As well as making them mean, money can make people greedy. The more they have, the more they want. They are always on the make, pushing morality to one side perhaps, overcharging for goods or services, underpaying their employees, taking the self-serving or exploitative route at every opportunity. Some people kill for money. Some old people have been murdered for their pensions! Even the old themselves can lose their mastery over money, becoming its victim rather that its owner, seeing it as something to be left intact and untouched – almost like an idol – because its their guarantee of some kind of a future or insurance against the rainy day. Yes, in many ways money can be a hugely negative factor in life. It is strange that a commodity which entered the system of exchange as a means should depreciate so quickly, in so many ways, and become an end in itself.

Our Lord praised the unjust steward in today's Gospel, not for being 'wasteful with his Master's property' (Lk 16:11), or for falsifying the accounts (Lk 16:5-7), but for having the foresight to secure his own future. If he looked after the boys, the boys would look after him. A little scratch of the pen in the interests of preservation! If the children of this world, Jesus is saying, are looking to their material future, then the children of light, his followers, should be looking to their spiritual future. No point in pleading when you come to the judgement that you weren't expecting it, that it came as a surprise! And we prepare for the judgement by using all our gifts, including money, not just for our own benefit, but for the benefit of others too, so that, in the words of Jesus, those with whom we have shared 'will welcome [us] into the tents of eternity' (Lk 16:9). Money is there for sharing; people are there to be helped. There is a battle in life between justice and injustice, between caring and not caring, between giving or adding it on! All of us have a fundamental choice to make as we journey towards eternity. We 'cannot be the slave both of God and of money' (Lk 16:13).

It would be wrong to give the impression that money as a force is entirely negative. Of course it isn't. Without it, we wouldn't have the houses in which we live, the schools to which we send our children, the hospitals to which we have recourse, the churches in which we pray. They all took money to build and it takes money to keep them going. Without money we couldn't send an astronaut into outer space or even a letter to America. When we use money to live and give our children a future or when we use it to create employment, for instance, we are doing something profoundly religious. Love of God means making life better for his children. Loving the neighbour translates sometimes into giving him a job. The prosperity we enjoy nowadays can be a great blessing provided it's imparted to all our people. One thing we need to watch though, in these affluent times, is what we do with our surplus. A fair slice of it should go to the poor. None of it should be set aside for showing off. Some of it already is! There is a growing tendency amongst us towards ostentation and pretentiousness. When money comes in on a high tide you always get a lot of froth. We can do without the froth. Money should go where it is needed. It should never go to the head. The money that is earned with honesty, used with generosity and spent with modesty is the finest currency of all.

Caring for the Poor

Amos 6:1, 4-7; 1 Tim 6:11-16; Lk 16:19-31

In 1984 there was a famine in Ethiopia. 800,000 people died. Forty years before that there was a famine in Bengal. The number of people who died was 3 million. In 1876–79 there was a famine in China. The death toll was appalling. Utterly appalling. The number who died was 13 million. The impression one gets from those figures is that things are improving. Perhaps they are in some places, but not nearly enough. Apart from the millions who are starving in the modern world, it is estimated that 900 million are on the edge of malnutrition. We are talking about now. The up-to-date, state-of-the-art now!

Most of the poverty in the world is in the southern hemisphere, in places like Africa and South America, for instance. Many of the countries in the southern hemisphere were colonised by the richer western powers that had little or nothing to learn about the white art of exploitation. Nowadays, former colonies are deeply in debt, grossly underdeveloped, naturally poor perhaps and particularly vulnerable to climatic excesses like typhoon or drought. If all that weren't bad enough, they are also lacking in the kind of support systems that we take for granted and that enable a people to survive and even thrive. By support systems, I mean water-schemes, irrigation, reserves of food, insurance, loan schemes, alternative employment and so on.

In 1987 there was a severe drought in the south-east of the US. No one died. They had support systems in place. They had reserves of food, irrigation, insurance and alternative employment. Yet, three years before, as we saw, 800,000 had died in Ethiopia. And three years later when the kind of drought that hit the States hit the Ethiopians they needed 1.3 million tons of emergency food to save the lives of 4 million people. If that hadn't come from abroad they were finished.

Or to give another example of the way these poorer countries are exposed. Farmers in the developing world must till their fields continuously. They cannot afford to give them a rest – to give the land time to recover. Fertilizers are very expensive; they are not easy to come by. The topsoil in these countries is often held in place by trees. But the people are so poor that they have to cut down the trees for firewood. And so along with the people, the trees themselves become the victims of poverty. Then the rains come and the topsoil is washed away. Then the land itself becomes the victim of poverty. In developing countries like that, subsistence agriculture is always on the brink of disaster.

In today's first reading, the prophet Amos paints a repulsive picture of the rulers of Judah and Israel, 'lying on their ivory beds, sprawling on their divans, stuffing themselves with stall fattened veal, guzzling wine by the bowlfull' (Amos 6:4-6) and not showing the slightest concern for their needy northern neighbours, referred to as 'Joseph', who was said to be their ancestor. Judah has no time for Joe. Not for the first time in human history are the indulgent indifferent to the poor. They are indifferent again in today's Gospel. The purple-clad rich man feasting magnificently has no conscience whatsoever about the starvation on the streets. This is the story of two worlds, distanced by immorality, unconnected by concern. The rich man that Jesus talks about is not just a reprehensible exception. He is one of a kind. He is a type or representative of all the rich who are callously and perhaps corpulently ensconced behind their high walls, while the dogs attend, in place of the humans, to the beggars at the gate. The Gospel then is about the gulf, symbolised by the gate, between the uncaring rich and the uncared-for poor.

THESE MIGHT HELP TOO

The challenge then of today's readings is first of all to the wealthier nations, including our own, to help the development of the poorer ones by increased financial aid, low-interest loans and the reduction or cancellation of existing debts. But there is a personal challenge in the readings for each one of us. We have reached the stage in this country now, happily enough, where, when we go out to eat, we have difficult choices to make, even with the starters, between stuffed mushrooms in garlic cream, crab claws with whatever you fancy and the grilled goats' cheese. In effect, we are lying on our ivory beds and sprawling on our divans. They don't even have the choice between life and death in the developing world. I know that recurring crises in different parts of Africa have the double effect of alerting and anaesthetising us at the same time. Recurring crises can become the norm – and the norm does not disturb. We need to be disturbed and we need to give until it hurts. Token offerings may meet our conscience but not starvation's need. When in John's Gospel Jesus was faced with five thousand hungry people, his question to Phillip was: 'where can we find some bread for these people to eat?' (Jn 6:5). You know yourselves what he did. So his message for us then was 'multiply the loaves'. He has the very same message for us today – albeit in different imagery. When the dogs in the street even know that the beggar is covered with sores, 'don't hide behind the gate'!

Increase Our Faith

Hab 1:2-3, 2:2-4; 2 Tim 1:6-8, 13-14; Lk 17:5-10

If I were to ask you this morning why you are practising your Christian faith, you'd probably say, 'I was born into it. It's my spiritual skin. And it fits me reasonably well'. Or you might say, 'I've seen the faith at work in the lives of my parents and what I saw impressed me. I'm impressed above all by Jesus himself – by his person and his teaching. I need a great love in my life along with the love of my family and he's it. And as well as being here in the present he's there in my future too as promised in his death and resurrection. I find myself in the flow of the faith and it is carrying me, if not past the cemetery, then hopefully beyond the grave'.

And if I were to ask you what forces are at work that tend to undermine your faith, you might say: 'the pace of change in a country that once stood still; the drift from the spiritual in the western world; the number of Catholics who have marginalised the Mass; the number of priests, if only a minority, who have been guilty of abuse.' Or you might say: 'the difficulties with faith in my life are coming from within, in a lack of motivation or a surrender to sin. There is a crumbling of my faith and all I'm doing is hanging in. I'm here in person now ostensibly but part of me isn't here at all.'

We are not the only ones who have difficulties in relation to faith or who have forces working against us. There is evidence in all three readings today that other people had difficulties as well. The prophet Habakuk's difficulty in the first reading was with the problem of evil. He was all the time wrestling with it. He is described as a 'wrestler with God'. What he couldn't understand was the randomness of suffering, the arbitrary nature of punishment as meted out by God. The particular problem that concerned him was the persecution of the people of Judah (his own people) by foreign invaders. Why did God permit that? If Judah was being punished for its sins – that, he could understand; but why should God use even greater sinners (the invaders) as agents of his punishment? 'How long, Lord, am I to cry for help,' he says, 'while you will not listen?' (Hab 1:2). St Paul's difficulty in the second reading wasn't an intellectual one like Habakuk's. He wasn't asking questions of God. But he knew as a preacher that God was asking questions of him. The big question God was asking was how much he was prepared to suffer. Paul was prepared to suffer anything – to be in prison (as he was then) or to be martyred (as he would be later). His worry was that his friend Timothy mightn't have the courage to do the same. In the Gospel, the difficulty the apostles had was that they couldn't cope with the demands of their faith. What they couldn't cope with in particular were the demands of forgiveness. Jesus had just told them in Luke 17:4 that no matter how often people sinned, provided they were repentant, forgiveness should be extended to them. The faith the apostles were supposed to practise left no room for resentment or retaliation at all. It was to be give, give, give all the time but give no kicks where you'd love to give them! It left you with no targets of any kind except the target of an all-embracing love.

Do the readings today come up with any answers for the people who had difficulties then and the people who have difficulties now? They do! Habakuk tells us, despite his own problems, that the most important thing is to be faithful. Keep faith in God – no matter what. 'The upright man will live by his faithfulness' (Hab 2:4). Paul is telling us much the same thing. We are 'never to be ashamed of witnessing to the Lord'. We are to put our faith 'in the power of God' and 'bear our hardships for the sake of the Good News' (2 Tim 1:8). Faith is not meant to be a passive inheritance. It's meant to be positive and proactive. Faith is meant not just to endure but to surmount – to energise and inspire! We may describe it as our spiritual skin but it was never meant to be an agent of containment, designed to inhibit and restrict us! We need to stir it up by living it, praying it, learning more about it, going to Church regularly, celebrating and cherishing the Eucharist. The apostles understood in today's Gospel that faith is for stretching, for responding, for growing. 'Increase our faith,' they said to Jesus, 'increase our faith' (Lk 17:5). Mindful of what they achieved and of what we might be able to achieve ourselves, but recognising our need of help, our constant need of help, we pray, with as much fervour as we can muster: 'Lord, increase our faith.'

Giving Thanks to God

2 Kings 5:14-17; 2 Tim 2:8-13; Lk 17:11-19

The incident in today's Gospel is astonishing. It is absolutely astonishing. What is astonishing about it is that nine of the ten people who were cured of their leprosy didn't bother to say 'thanks'. They were healed of everything but their ingratitude. They had a disease of the heart that they didn't recognise at all. A by-pass wouldn't have helped them, whatever about a transplant. Naaman, from the first reading, could have helped them, if they followed his example. When he was cured by Elisha, he had the decency to come back with a gift. He knew what he owed. The Samaritan in the Gospel could have helped them as well, if only they had followed in his footsteps. All they do in the Gospel is disappear. 'Where are they?' Jesus asked, 'Where are they?' (Lk 17:18). How could they forget so quickly? How could they fail to acknowledge their indebtedness? They weren't so shy in coming forward! Why were they so slow to come back?

The failure of the nine to say 'thanks' becomes all the more inexplicable when you consider the predicament from which they had been delivered. They were plucked by Jesus from the jaws of hell. Here were people on the outer edges of isolation. Here were people who had no future as human beings at all. The only future that was left to them was to consort with their own kind and call in desperation to a world that had abandoned them. In the Bible, leprosy covered a range of skin diseases. Its worst form, now known as Hansen's disease, led to a thickening and discoloration of the skin, extensive ulceration, deformity of the hands and feet and disfigurement of the face. Worst of all, it led to the disfigurement of your life. Once you became a leper you had to leave. Not only were you diseased in the eyes of the Jews, worst of all in their perception of things you were defiled. Your continuing presence in the community would be a defilement of others. The fate you'd have to endure was spelled out in the book of Leviticus without any concession to compassion. 'A man infected with leprosy must wear his clothing torn and his hair disordered; he must shield his upper lip and cry, "Unclean, Unclean". As long as the disease lasts he must be unclean; and therefore he must live apart; he must live outside the camp' (Lev 13:45-46). In view of that sentence, I suppose one could say in defence of the nine ungrateful lepers that the experience of being outcasts had led, not just to the disordering of their hair, but to the disordering of normal human responses as well. The leprosy had led not only to the thickening of their skins but to the coarsening of their sensibilities. They were treated as aliens by their own people. They had become the casualties of an alien world.

What we need to watch is that we don't become casualties of an alien world ourselves, a world of coarsened sensibilities, where gratitude is either not felt or not shown. A world where there is no word in the vocabulary for 'thanks'. What we need to do is to take our cue from the grateful Samaritan rather than the ungrateful nine. The Samaritan may have been of mixed race, but there is nothing mixed about his message. He is reminding us in the clearest possible terms to be grateful to God. This is what he was himself! 'Finding himself cured,' the Gospel tells us, '[he] turned back praising God at the top of his voice ... threw himself at the feet of Jesus and thanked him' (Lk 17:15-16). His response wasn't just a human response, it was a faith response as well. He wasn't just grateful, he was believing. He gave the ultimate credit to God. He realised that God was compassionately and generously present in what Jesus had done for him. Naaman realised the same thing in what the God of Israel had done for him through the

THESE MIGHT HELP TOO

prophet Elisha. This God would be his God for ever more! He would offer him sacrifices on the holy soil of Israel which his two mules would bring home for him. And he himself would be 'mulishly' grateful to God for the rest of his life. The clear message from today's readings then is 'thanks be to God'.

How are we to show our gratitude to God? By praising him at the top of our voices like the Samaritan! By retaining our sense of wonder. By celebrating the abundance of his creation and his longing for our salvation. By keeping his commandments of course. By using our talents in the service of his people. By adding to an awareness of his presence in our concern for the suffering and the poor. By offering him sacrifice on holy ground like Naaman. That is what we are trying to do together now. That is what we try to do together every Sunday. A stubborn attachment to our community Mass has a lot to recommend it! God will be the last to complain of in that particular respect – we grow up to be a mule!

Persistence in Prayer

Ex 17:8-13; 2 Tim 3:14-4:2; Lk 18:1-8

When I was twelve or thirteen years old my parents sent me on a message to Ballaghadereen. Just as I was boarding the bus in my native Charlestown, a local business man who loved a flutter asked me to put a £5 win and £2 place on a horse in the Steward's Cup called 'Blue Butterfly'. His odds were thirty-three to one. The winnings would come to around £200, which was a small fortune in those days. A few hours later, I was at a counter in Ballaghadereen when I heard the race on the radio. 'Blue Butterfly' was flying at the head of the field and the bet was still in my pocket. In panic, I started to pray: 'Please Lord don't let him win! Don't let him win.' But winning he still was, streaking towards the finish, kicking his heels up at heaven. I prayed and prayed again. The winning post was coming closer with every stride. Then with fifty yards to go and another anguished burst of prayer, a wall of horses came sweeping into contention and in a final flourish of short heads 'Blue Butterfly' was fourth. I breathed a huge sigh of relief. I looked around the shop but there was no one to share my deliverance with except God. I don't know whether he remembers this or not but I thanked him very much! I really did!

Was I right to thank him? Had he been listening to my prayer? Would 'Blue Butterfly' have lost in any event? Was the horse's defeat due to his own inadequacy or were other punters praying with greater fervour for the horse that eventually won? Was God involved in the thing at all? I raise the question in a frivolous way, in a sporting context, not because I'm worried about the answer to it, but because it masks a serious concern about the efficacy of prayer in areas of far greater consequence. When it comes

THESE MIGHT HELP TOO

to life and death matters, prayers of petition, seeking a particular outcome, do not seem to work a lot of the time! We all know that. Blue Butterflies go on to win in our world and leave us to pick up the pieces. Barring miracles, some diseases with which we are familiar plough on relentlessly to their virulent little victories and leave us heartbroken in their wake. There is meanness in our world that knows nothing of compassion and is impervious to petition. It seems to pick its victims for maximum suffering with indiscriminate malevolence. There are so many random afflictions in our everyday experience that they would demolish your faith in prayer.

In today's first reading, as long as Moses kept his arms up in prayer, his people got the better of the Amalekites. As soon as he dropped his arms, as soon as he got weak in the elbows, his people began to lose ground. Persistence in prayer! In the Gospel of St Luke today, the widow got vindication from the judge, not because he was just, but because she herself was persevering. She just wouldn't leave him alone. Persistence in prayer again. In the parable of 'the friend at midnight' the man who came knocking at the door got his three loaves eventually, not because he was in need, but because his knocking made him a nuisance. He'd stay there knocking for the night (Lk 11:5-8). Persistence in prayer yet again. Now, anything the judge will do, God himself will do better. Anything the owner of the loaves will do, God will do better as well. Their motive was to get rid of people. God's desire is to help us out. What these people did in their own interest, God will do in ours. That's what Jesus is saying to us in the telling of these stories. He spelled it out in the clearest possible terms (Lk 11:9-11) when he said, 'Ask, and it will be given to you; search, and you will find; knock and the door will be opened to you. For the one who asks always receives; the one who searches always finds; the one who knocks always has the door opened to him'.

What Jesus is saying doesn't mean that we'll get exactly what we ask for, every time we ask for it – or even the only time we ask for it. Our persistence in prayer is not the only factor in the ordering of the universe, any more than a child's persistence is the only factor in the dispositions of a family. I was in a house lately where a young girl was readying herself for what I can only describe as a 'petitionary onslaught' on her parents. At only eleven years of age she was shaping up for their permission to go to her first disco! The request was evident in her body language before she had said anything at all. Nothing held her attention for long. She stirred uneasily in her chair, moved restlessly from room to room, pulling drawers out and shoving them in again in her anxiety to find an opening. When she made her first probe into her parents' defences it was met with a strategy of containment. Try as she might and no matter how long she persisted she never managed to break through. But she was getting an answer all the same, not the one she wanted to hear, but the one her parents thought best for her. Her welfare was best reflected in their will rather than in her wilfulness. She has continued and will continue to cherish her parents and to put her faith in them because she knows that they love her. Despite God's apparent rejection of us at times and the terrible crosses we may have to bear, we must continue to persist in our prayers and in our faith because we know that he loves us too. Nobody loves us more and has our best interests at heart than the one who died for us on the cross and rose for us from the dead. Today's readings are an encouragement to us to trust in God, in the same way that, as children, we trusted in our parents. 'But when the Son of Man comes,' Jesus asked, 'will he find any faith on earth?' (Lk 18:8). We pray that when he comes for us, whatever about our false starts and our many failures, we won't be found wanting in faith!

The Pharisee and the Publican

Eccles (Sir) 35:12-14, 16-19; 2 Tim 4:6-8, 16-18; Lk 18:9-14

If I were a Pharisee in Our Lord's time, I'd feel very aggrieved about the way I had been depicted in today's Gospel. I'd nearly be inclined to take libel action. The portrait we get of the Pharisee is entirely negative – even misleading. It gives the impression that there is little or nothing to be said for Pharisees in general. That, quite simply, is not the case. Pharisaism as a philosophy and a movement was earnest and well meaning. It came into existence at the beginning of the second century BC as a separatist impulse, to preserve the Jewish faith in its entirety and to protect the people of God from pagan contamination by gentiles, sinners and non-observant Jews. It was at once a defensive reaction – a circling of the wagons if you like – but a positive force for conservation as well. Most members of the Pharisaic movement were lay people who weren't getting the spiritual leadership they needed from a self-indulgent priesthood, and who had no option, they felt, but to take the law into their own hands. The law in question was the Torah, the written law as given by God to Moses, but the oral law as well, the interpretations of the written law as handed on to them by their fathers. The Pharisees were traditionalists. They were sticklers for the law – not because they saw it as an imposition but because they experienced it as a way of life which determined everything they did, down to the smallest detail.[1] The Pharisees weren't just traditionalists. They were miniaturists as well. They were microscopic in their approach – especially when it came to Sabbath observance, ritual washing and the paying of tithes. No infraction of law was to be tolerated, not even the plucking of ears of corn on the Sabbath (Mk 2:23). No detail was to be overlooked. You had to serve the Lord your God, not only in life's sweeping sentences, but in all the brackets of life as well. They could claim, and rightly claim, to have some wonderful people among their members. As evidence of that, they could point to Nicodemus, who brought a mixture of myrrh and aloes to prepare the body of Jesus for burial (Jn 19:39). They could point to Joseph of Arimathaea, who wrapped the body in a shroud and laid it in the tomb (Lk 23:53). They could point, most of all to St Paul, who made more of the empty tomb than any other preacher in history. The Pharisees aren't to be written off completely. They had their good points too!

If I were a Pharisee in Our Lord's time, I'd feel very aggrieved, not only by the caricature of the Pharisee in today's Gospel but by the flattering portrait of the Publican. The publicans (Latin word for tax collectors) weren't as harmless and inoffensive as the portrait suggests. They were public predators who collected taxes for the Romans or their minions, sent only a percentage of what they collected to the authorities and kept a handsome surplus for themselves. They were 'outcasts' among their own people because of their greedy and rapacious ways, their contact with 'unclean' pagans and their collaboration with the occupying powers. The fellow in today's Gospel gets credit for staying at the back of the temple. With the record of dishonesty he was bound to have brought with him, he had a nerve to go into the temple at all. So enough of this ill-considered comparison! Please spare us the vanquishment of the Pharisee by the Publican!

Despite all that has been said, and there is a lot of truth in what has been said, the comparison, or rather the contrast, is valid. The trouble with the Pharisees, or some of them at least, is that in their self-conscious observance of the law they became insufferably self-righteous. Morally and spiritually they became a pain in the neck! The Pharisee in today's parable is a prime example. Recall for a moment the way he conducted himself. He raised himself to his full height, set himself apart from and above the rest of the human race, arched his neck like a swan, listed the sins from which he had refrained, enumerated the virtues he had put into practice and put all the daylight in the temple between himself and the tax collector. He was perfection itself. The law had reached its consummation in him. Even God must have been a little bit surprised! What the Pharisee didn't do at all – and this is quite extraordinary – he didn't ask for anything! He didn't feel the need of anything. He was sufficiency itself. He was presenting himself to God as gift! The tax collector, by contrast, knew he was a gift to nobody. He had spent his life gifting himself at other people's expense. For reasons other than self-preservation he was keeping his head down now. He felt so ashamed and remorseful that he couldn't even look God in the eye. He made no attempt whatsoever at exoneration or self-justification. He was, in his own estimation, an out-and-out sinner in need of forgiveness. With a humility honed by repeated failure and years of self-loathing perhaps, he gave voice to his feelings of total dependence. What he needed more than anything else in his life was his God. 'God, be merciful to me, a sinner' (Lk 18:14). That God would indeed be merciful is the assurance we get from Jesus. 'This man, I tell you, went home again at rights with God; the other did not' (Lk 18:14). What was true in the parable of the Pharisee and the Publican remains true for us. The repentant rather than the self-righteous are the ones who are close to God. Before we go home today from this particular temple, perhaps we'll find cause in our conscience as to why we should beat our breasts.

Note

1. See Sean Freyne, *The World of the New Testament*, Michael Glazier, 1980.

Calling All Sinners

Wis 11:22-12:2; 2 Thess 1:11-2:2; Lk 19:1-10

If there is one thing that becomes increasingly clear as we read through the Gospels, it is that our Lord had an awful lot of time for tax collectors and sinners. He knew himself that the people regarded him as their friend (Mt 11:19). And the people were right. We read in Mark, chapter two, for instance, that 'when Jesus was at dinner in his own house, a number of tax collectors and sinners were also sitting at the table ... for there were many of them among his followers' (Mk 2:15). He was so partial to tax collectors that very early on in his ministry he called one of them, Levi, to be among his chosen disciples (Mk 2:15). Last Sunday, when the Pharisee and the tax collector (or publican) were engaged in what you might describe as a 'prayer contest', he gave the verdict decisively to the tax collector (Lk 18:14). Then to cap it all today, even though there were crowds of people all round him on the ground, he went to the trouble of calling another tax collector, Zacchaeus, down from the tree because he wanted to dine in his house (Lk 19:5). I suppose from our perspective he wasn't doing anything out of the ordinary at all.

As far as the people around him were concerned, he certainly was. And they weren't one bit impressed. You could go as far as to say that they were deeply resentful. When they were looking up at Zacchaeus in the sycamore tree what do you think was in their minds? Well, some were hoping he'd stay up there! The rest of them were hoping he'd fall down and break his neck! All of them were upset that Jesus was going to break bread with him. 'He has gone to stay,' they said, 'at a sinners house' (Lk 19:7).

Well, weren't they all sinners? Were they being self-righteous? No, they weren't! A sinner for them wasn't

THESE MIGHT HELP TOO

somebody who sinned occasionally or even regularly. Their 'sinners' were really wicked people who lived outside the law, had no time for God, preyed on the poor and made a fortune for themselves. Sinners like that included tax gatherers, because their profession gave them the opportunity and their history the habit of ripping off everybody in sight. Sin was one thing and understandable. Wickedness was systematic and reprehensible. You could fall into one and glory in the other. Glorying was a sin too far!

Now, there were at least two types of tax gatherer. First of all, there was the fellow who collected the tribute for Rome. He would demand from the people more than he was obliged to send away and then grow fat on the surplus. One such parasite was a man called Capito. The Jewish philosopher Philo wrote around AD 40: 'Capito is the tax collector for Judea and cherishes a spite against the population. When he came there he was a poor man, but by his rapacity and peculation he has amassed much wealth in various forms!'[1] A second type of tax gatherer was a customs officer. That's what Zacchaeus was. The Gospel says 'he was one of the senior tax collectors and a wealthy man' (Lk 19:2). The inference is clear. His wealth had come from his 'personal take' out of the duties charged on exports and imports. As long as trading continued, Zacchaeus would do well. He might have to climb a tree for a view when Jesus was passing by, but he'd never have to climb for a shekel. They tumbled into his lap from the pockets of the poor in a manner that classified him as 'wicked'. The fact that Jesus would go out of his way to dine with such a man didn't just upset the people or make them angry. It gave them considerable offence. They would have felt abandoned, even betrayed.

Why did Jesus risk alienating these people? Why didn't he keep his distance from tax collectors and sinners? Because he came on earth on a mission of rescue! Because he came not to exclude anybody but to save all! His special concern was to save those of us who had gone astray! That's what he said himself when he was asked about it! 'It is not the healthy who need the doctor,' he said, 'but the sick. I did not come to call the virtuous but sinners' (Mk 2:17). He said the same thing about the lost sheep. He'd 'leave the ninety-nine in the wilderness and go after the missing one until he found it' (Lk 15:4). He said it yet again in relation to Zacchaeus. 'For the son of man has come to seek out and save what was lost' (Lk 19:10). Jesus didn't just set out to dine with Zacchaeus, he set out to convert him. And convert him he did! The man would 'give half his property to the poor' and 'four times' what he had stolen (Lk 19:8). All the law required was that he pay back what he had taken, add twenty per cent as a fine and sacrifice a ram as a guilt offering (Lev 1:7). Zacchaeus went much further than that! What Jesus accomplished in Zacchaeus, he wants to accomplish in us. He loves us for our own sake, as he loved the tax collectors and sinners, but he wants us to be better. What he wants most of all from us, if we've gone astray, is a complete change of heart. Down from our perch we have to come and break bread with Jesus at the table. Break with our past too and give up our immoral ways. That's the challenge and that's the opportunity. But it is a wonderful opportunity. Zacchaeus may have been a small man but he was big enough to grasp it. Are we big enough? And humble enough? Do we or do we not want to hear Jesus say what he said to the repentant Zacchaeus? 'Today salvation has come to this house' (Lk 19:9).

Note
1.   E.P. Sanders, *The Historical Figure of Jesus*, Penguin, 1996, p. 228.

Resurrection and the
Message of Spring

2 Macc 7:1-2, 9-14; 2 Thess 2:16-3:5; Lk 20:27-38

Maybe I shouldn't say this, but the older I get and the nearer I come to the grave, the harder it is to believe in a personal resurrection. Indeed, the harder it is to believe in an afterlife at all. When people are young and full of vitality and part of a growing company they can envisage all kinds of futures – including resurrection. Resurrection is part of the long road. But when the road shortens and our circle begins to shrink, we become more conscious of closure in this life and less confident of a resumption. The only life with which we are familiar is characterised by transience and conclusion. Our future is with the fallen leaves, the winter tells us, already coffined in their own colours. No point in taking refuge in illusion. Others will take our places in the spring.

Why have I begun with such a gloomy paragraph? Because it's the way some people feel at times and because it's the kind of paragraph with which the Sadducees in today's Gospel would sympathise. As far as they were concerned, our future would be with the fallen leaves, because they didn't believe in an afterlife at all, much less a bodily resurrection. In order to reduce the notion of a bodily resurrection to absurdity, they presented Jesus with a marital conundrum or marital tangle. The Law of Moses stipulated in Deut 25:5 that if a man married and died childless, his brother should marry the widow, have children with her hopefully, so that the first-born son could carry on the dead man's name. Now in a situation where seven brothers, in turn, married the same woman, without having a child, which of them would be the good lady's husband in the life to come? Smart as they were now, their conundrum confounded nobody. It certainly didn't confound Jesus. There would be no marital tangle in the next life for the simple reason that there would be no marriage. Heaven wasn't going to be a reactivated earth, if that is what the Sadducees were insinuating. The life we have here wasn't going to be taken 'body and bones' and replicated in heaven. The risen life would be a new experience where people would be 'the same as the angels' in their relationship with one another and with God (Lk 20:36).

The wonderful thing about today's Gospel is not that Jesus got the better of the Sadducees but that he emphasised for us the reality of an afterlife and a resurrection. He did that in three ways: firstly, by rejecting the effort to reduce it to absurdity; secondly, by stressing that risen life is a new kind of bodily existence, along the lines of the 'spiritual body' that St Paul talks about later in I Cor 15:35; and thirdly, by quoting Ex 3:6 where God, speaking to Moses, says 'I am the God of your father ... the God of Abraham, the God of Isaac, the God of Jacob'. Now, these three Jewish patriarchs were dead. But God was talking in the present tense. 'I am their God now', he was saying. The clear implication is that they are certainly alive, if not yet risen. Jesus himself gives substance to that interpretation when he says at the end of today's Gospel, 'Now he is God, not of the dead, but of the living; for to him all men are in fact alive' (Lk 20:38). So the second brother of the Maccabees wasn't far wrong in the first reading when he said 'the King of the world will raise us up – to live again forever' (2 Macc 7:9).

So whenever I have doubts about the reality of an after life or a bodily resurrection, I recall what Jesus said to the Sadducees and it helps to reassure me. I recall what he said on other occasions as well – especially what he is quoted as saying to Martha in John's Gospel, before the raising of Lazarus; 'I am the Resurrection. If anyone believes in me, even though he dies, he will live, and whoever lives and believes in me will never die' (Jn 11:26). There is an even clearer reference to resurrection in John, chapter six where Jesus is quoted as saying, 'Anyone who does eat my flesh and drink my blood has eternal life, and I will raise him up on the last day' (Jn 6:14). What I find most compelling of all is Christ's own resurrection and the promise within it for us. Of all the events in history, it is the one with the greatest future. It is the Easter glory released in Christ that all of us bring to our graves. What happened to him in the Resurrection will also happen to us. It couldn't be a question of his victory and our failure. It has to be a question of his victory and our victory too! We know from the empty tomb that we are not on an empty journey. With the outline of our destiny before us, we are following in his wake. St Paul put all that very well when he wrote, 'Christ … has been raised from the dead, the first fruits of all who have fallen asleep … Just as all men die in Adam so all men will be brought to life in Christ. Christ as the first fruits and then, after the coming of Christ, those who belong to him' (1 Cor 15:20-23). Our future is with the fallen leaves, the winter tells us. Our future is in the first fruits, is the message of spring!

Endurance

Mal 3:19-20; 2 Thess 3:7-12; Lk 21:5-19

We were standing in the car park beside St Michael's Church in Ballinasloe, watching the roof above the sanctuary going up in flames. Here was a beautiful building in danger of being burned to the ground. If that were to happen, the loss to the local population and our architectural heritage would be incalculable. The Church, which owed its design to two celebrated architects McCarthy and Pugin, had been widely recognised as 'one of the most distinguished and satisfying examples of neo-Gothic building in nineteenth-century Ireland'.[1] It had been dedicated to an Archangel in the Heavens but it belonged in a very special way to the poorer inhabitants of the earth in the Ballinasloe area who had been largely responsible for putting it up. As the black smoke thickened towards the sky, we prayed as we never prayed before and put our faith in St Michael and the fire brigade. If the Church was totally destroyed, it would be, for the immediate future anyway, the end of the world.

On three occasions in their history the Jewish people had to watch their temple being razed to the ground. The first temple they saw destroyed was the Temple of Solomon. That event took place when invaders from Babylon laid waste the entire city of Jerusalem in 586 BC. When they returned from exile in Babylon seventy years later, the tenacious Jewish people built a second temple, smaller in size, but larger in loyalty to their only God, Yahweh. For three hundred and fifty years this temple was the centre of their national life. It was the goal of their pilgrimages and the object of their love. It meant more to them than any other building in Palestine. Yet, for a second time a generation of Jewish people had to watch helplessly while a fire, this time instigated by the Greeks, licked expectantly at the pillars of their hallowed shrine. A third generation of Jews would see the same kind of thing happen again. The man who would rebuild the temple the third time was Herod the Great. The pillagers who would reduce it to rubble would be the Romans. The year was AD 70. The early Christians whom Luke is writing to in today's Gospel thought it was the end of the world, not just in the metaphorical sense or for the immediate future, but in the strictly literal sense and for all time! As with the temple, so with the world! Things were coming to an end.

In order to make it clear to the early Christians that things weren't coming to an end, that the end of the world wasn't round the corner, Luke took his readers back in today's Gospel to an earlier discussion between Jesus and his disciples. In the course of that discussion, when Jesus foretold that the temple would be destroyed, his followers wondered whether the end of the temple would signify the end of Time! No, it would not, Jesus assured them! It would be one of many cataclysmic events in the course of their lives – like famines and earthquakes and wars. The road ahead would be difficult for all of them. Some of the daunting events that lay ahead would include persecution for themselves and even betrayal for some of them by members of their own families. The temple of their own lives, if you like, would be taken down stone by stone. Christ's message, however, wasn't one of foreboding but of forbearance. Indeed, it was much more positive than that. They were to face the future not just with forbearance but with fortitude. If such fortitude was forthcoming they would be given the wisdom they needed to cope with their difficulties and even if the ultimate misfortune befell them and they had to die for his sake, to die in such a cause was not to perish. The radiant side of martyrdom was reward. On no account would their sacrifice go unrewarded. Their endurance would win them their lives (Lk 21:19).

One of the lessons for us from today's Gospel is that life is bound to be difficult for modern Christians as well. Apart from appalling disasters like tsunamis or famines which are indiscriminately destructive, there are forces at work which are destructive of the Church as such, some of them self-inflicted, as, for instance, when adult evil preys upon youthful innocence, leaving a legacy of hurt and cynicism in its wake. Calamities like that, whatever their nature, are bound to test our faith. Then there are the personal difficulties that all of us are liable to encounter, the relationships that break down, the death of those we love, the failure to achieve in life the role we envisioned in our youth, the shrinking of our social circle as the years go by, the consignment to the margins as we drift into old age. Any one of these experiences can put pressure on our faith. Faith and disenchantment don't rest easily together. That's why today's Gospel encourages fortitude in ourselves and fidelity to Christ.

Always at this time of year I'm reminded of my childhood when my mother would be rearing young turkeys for the Christmas. They were known as 'bronze' turkeys, which aptly described their colour but hardly their constitution. They were the most delicate creatures you ever came across and the hardest to rear. The disaster confronting them was a disease known as 'the peck'. As soon as it assailed them, they gave in, seemingly without a fight, and 'let their wings down'. Today's Gospel makes no concessions to 'the peck'. No Christian is to 'let the wings down' or give in without a fight. In spiritual terms, the 'pecking order' for the Christian, if not the poor turkey, is endurance first and survival later. We are to strive to be 'bronze' not just in colour or in name but in constancy and in character. Jesus himself was putting it far more elegantly but conveying roughly the same message when he said, 'Your endurance will win you your lives'.

Note

1.   Patrick K. Egan, *The Parish of Ballinasloe*, Dublin: Clonmore and Reynold Ltd, 1959, p. 246.

THESE MIGHT HELP TOO

Christ the King

2 Sam 5:1-3; Col 1:12-20; Lk 23:35-43

When I was a student in Maynooth long ago and the year came to an end – just before Christmas – a fleet of buses used to come out from Dublin to the college to take us back into the city so that we could catch the trains to our different destinations. The buses would arrive at seven in the morning. We'd be up at about five, levitating with excitement because we were leaving the year behind and heading for home. One lad was so excited that he nailed his chamber pot – an enamel chamber pot – to the middle of the floor in his room. He never came back. The authorities nailed him. The first place some of us would head for in Dublin was the Castle Hotel because for half-a-crown, or 15 cents now, we'd get a big fry there, mounded like a plum pudding, the first fry we'd have seen for nearly four months. The journey home on the train was an experience of sustained elation paralleled by the rhythm of the wheels. Our joy would reach its climax when we walked in the door at home to be reunited with our parents and family. We had survived the year – we had another year under our belt and Christmas was up ahead.

Well, today is the last Sunday of the Church's year and although we don't have the surging excitement that we used to experience as students, there should be some sense of celebration in our lives as well. We have survived another year. The wheel has gone full circle again and we're still here. That's something to be thankful for! For the work we were able to do, the friendship we enjoyed, the celebrations that we had and the difficulties we have overcome we give thanks first of all to the Lord. And that's precisely what the Church invites us to do this day. She points us to the Castle where our heavenly king resides. She says to all her children: turn now at the climax of the year and give grateful recognition to Christ your King.

The kings and queens with whom we are familiar don't have a great deal of personal authority. The authority they enjoy is symbolic rather than real. They cut tapes, visit hospitals, attract tourists, represent their country abroad, provide a pivotal presence around which the national life can revolve. But they don't die for us as Christ did, as today's readings remind us. They don't rise for us, as he did. They don't live on through the generations in word and sacrament and eucharist as he does. They are not our saviour, our teacher, our first and foremost friend. The territory over which they preside may be far-flung and extensive. The territory he wants from us is the territory of the heart. He calls each one of us not just to citizenship but to discipleship. He calls each one of us into a deep, intimate, personal relationship that will make enormous demands on us at times in terms of sacrifice, but that will lead inevitably to a corresponding and compensating joy! 'If anyone wants to be a follower of mine, let him renounce himself, take up his cross and follow me. For anyone who wants to save his life will lose it, but anyone who loses his life for my sake will find it' (Mt 16:24-25). What this king of ours demands is total commitment, an allegiance that may falter at times but that should never be allowed to fail.

So let's be practical now for a moment! Next Sunday is the beginning of Advent. It's a season of preparation for the coming of our king. It's an excellent opportunity to show our allegiance. We will meet Christ, between now and Christmas, first of all in the poor. This king of ours is never dressed in royal robes. Very often he's in rags. He is inner city king, lower income king, king of skimping lives and threadbare places. If at this time of year he reminds us of his presence in the poor, it's not only in the stable of his birth, but in the hovels of our heedlessness and negligence. We

THESE MIGHT HELP TOO

are being reproached by Christ at Christmas, and coaxed to generosity as well. You have been generous before. When he rattles the collection box and calls us to a wider justice, you'll be generous again. I know you will!

Finally, between now and Christmas, we'll meet Jesus, not only in the poor, but in our prayer as well. Ordinary kings may be entitled to our respect. This king of ours is entitled to our worship. So let's meet him on our knees, in our room, with the family, in the local community, here in Church. There can be a thinning of congregations on Advent Sundays because people have taken off to some temple other than this one. Some trading temple I mean, where people are worshipping at the shelves, I'm afraid, rather than at the shrines. I know there is a lot of shopping to be done. And I don't underestimate the pressure on people. But a spiritual feast calls for some prayerful preparation. Please don't lose sight of that! The person whose birthday we'll be celebrating is 'the image of the unseen God' (Col 1:15). 'He made it possible for us to join the saints and with them to inherit the light' (Col 1:12). Let's not be blind to that. In our generosity to the poor and the fervour of our prayer, let's give a right royal welcome to Christ our King

Other Feasts
and
Occasions

The Undivided Mary

Gen 3:9-15; 20; Eph 1:3-6; 11-12; Lk 1:26-38

The practices we have of putting a vase of flowers before a statue or a lighted candle before a holy picture or genuflecting before the Blessed Sacrament are instinctual. There is something similarly instinctual about the timing of today's feast. Here it is on 8 December, perfectly placed in the run-up to Christmas. It isn't so much that the mother is expecting a baby. It's that there are certain expectations for the mother and of the mother because of the baby itself. Flowers before the statue, the candle before the picture, the genuflection before the Blessed Sacrament; the Immaculate Conception before Christmas Day. There is something intuitive here. The placing is just right. We'll come back to it.

You know already what the Immaculate Conception means. It means that from the moment of her conception in her mother's womb, Mary was preserved from original sin. She was redeemed by her son as all of us were. She wasn't a goddess, she was a human being, but Christ's act of redemption was by way of prevention. Where we were cleansed, she was spared. She had 'won God's favour' from the start (Lk 1:28). Of all the creatures who have ever lived, she was the only one to be born immaculate. Why? What's at the root of all this?

The timing of today's feast has already suggested the answer, for the simple and wonderful reason that she was to be God's mother. And God's mother had to be very special. I mean, you don't give a chipped cup to a visitor. You don't give a soiled soother to a baby. You don't use instruments in an operation without making sure that they are perfectly clean. You prepare them. You don't choose a creature to be your mother without preparing her. That's what God did. He conferred every privilege on Mary that he possibly could. He left nothing to chance and certainly left nothing to Satan. He didn't let evil get a toehold on Mary even for an instant. 'I will make you enemies of each other; you and the woman, your offspring and her offspring' (Gen 3:15). In his beautiful prose-poem, the French writer Henri Godin explores the divine attitude very well. He has God the Father speaking and saying: 'And when I sent my Son on earth, he was not hard to please ... either about food or lodging or state of life or anything ... except his mother. But about her he was exacting. He wanted his mother to be a masterpiece ... and men are like him. Choosing a woman is always the great affair of their life. "Which doesn't surprise me," says God.' Godin tells us that choosing Mary was the great affair of God's life. He couldn't afford to get it wrong. And he didn't.

There is none of us immaculate. Original sin has got a good old grip on all of us. We can be very weak and sinful at times and when sinfulness gets the upper hand we tend to hide even from ourselves. We live in a make-believe world, unwilling to recognise who and what we are. We become the author of our own duality – two persons living uneasily side by side. We prefer to live with the fictional version of ourselves rather than with the divided reality we have become. There is none of us, I think, who doesn't, at one time or another, put distance between ourselves and our conscience. We take refuge in flight. This hiding from ourselves of course is really a hiding from God. We think so little of ourselves that we don't want to think of him at all. For the present anyway and to still our consciences, we'd prefer to scrub him out of existence. His presence is so disturbing that we try to keep ahead of him all the time – so far ahead in fact that he'll be minded to give up the chase. The poet Frances Thompson describes a similar attempt at flight in his poem 'The Hound of Heaven': 'I fled him down

THESE MIGHT HELP TOO

the nights and down the days; I fled him down the arches of the years; I fled him down the labyrinthine ways of my own mind and in the midst of tears, I hid from him.'

Now, today's feast is telling us to stop running because it reminds us that the Immaculate Mary didn't run from God. We cannot separate the role for which Mary was prepared from the manner in which she fulfilled it. There was no flight from God in her life and no duality in her response. And let's not be discouraged either by the superior quality of that response and her apparent self-sufficiency. Perfect models can be too much for imperfect mortals! We know that! But even if we cannot find a chink in Mary's discipleship, we can take comfort and huge encouragement from her humility. As far as she was concerned, it wasn't what she had achieved for God but what God had achieved in her. She spelled it out for us in her 'Magnificat': 'For the almighty has done great things for me. Holy is his name' (Lk 1:49). If only we would put our trust in God as Mary did, and confront our sinfulness rather than run away from it, the Almighty would be only too happy to do great things for us too. In that sense, may he do great things for you and me in the year to come.

Present Lives

Mal 3:1-4; Heb 2:14-18; Lk 2:22-40

If you were a Jew in Our Lord's time and you were blessed with your first child and he happened to be a boy, you'd go up to the temple in Jerusalem and present him to the Lord. And the presentation you'd make would be based on the notion of possession. As a pious Jew, it would be your conviction that your first born was possessed by God, belonged to God in a very special way. So you'd bring five shekels with you – a week's wages – to buy him back to settle your account. And if you were a poor person and couldn't afford any more, you'd make an additional offering on behalf of the mother – a pair of turtle doves. Not only would you give thanks to God but you'd give him his due. You'd feel freer now in your relationship with your son. He was yours with God's blessing at birth of course, but yours again now with a slap of the hand at the presentation. A done deal! Honour had been satisfied on both sides. God had given you a son and you had given him something for himself. The work of the day was done. I know I'm not doing them justice but it was against that kind of background that Mary and Joseph presented their child Jesus to the Lord. There would have been a fullness in their day, the kind of fullness you may have experienced yourself when you brought your child for baptism.

Full as their day was in terms of acknowledging and offering and giving, there was more to their presentation than that. It was an experience of revelation. It was part of their discovery that this child was not merely the light of their eyes but also the light of the world. Did you notice that all through the Christmas season the image that dominated the readings was the image of darkness and light? 'The people that walked in darkness have seen a great light. On those who live in a land of deep shadow, a light has shone' (Is 9:2). And again, 'all that came to be had life in him and that life was the light of men – a light that shines in the dark – a light that darkness could not overpower' (Jn 1:4-5). The light motif occurs so often that what we've had since Christmas is a festival of light. And today is the final day. Today is the day when Simeon of the second sight, the devout old man who had been in and out of the temple all his life, by some extraordinary intuition under the guidance of the Spirit recognised in Jesus the Messiah his people had been waiting for. He took the child in his arms and said, 'Now Master, you can let your servant go in peace, for my eyes have seen the salvation which you have prepared for all the nations to see – a light to enlighten the pagans and the glory of your people Israel' (Lk 2:29-32). It was a wonderful moment. 'A moment when the world's old age welcomed into its arms the eternal youth of God.'[1] A candle like that one there exists for one reason only – to give off light. It's not the only source of light that we have. Nor is it the primary source. But in the Christian tradition it draws attention to the primary source and symbolises it. So the feast of the Presentation has its effulgent or luminous side. It is also the feast of Candlemas. Today, we bless and light our candles to celebrate the presence in our midst of Jesus, the light of the world.

Is there anything else we should do today to celebrate this feast? I think there is! I think we should do what Mary and Joseph did – present our babies, our children and young people to God and ask for a special blessing on them. Even though Joseph and Mary bought their child back from God, they didn't own him. He would go his own way, carry out his own mission, reminding them when he was only twelve years old that 'he had to be busy with his Father's affairs' (Lk 2:50). We don't own our children either. They will go their own way too. But we pray fervently today that their way will be Christ's way, that they will welcome the baby Jesus into their arms, into their own generation as Simeon did into his. We pray too for ourselves, for Christ our light didn't mean to keep the light for himself. He meant us to reproduce it and reflect it. 'You are the light of the world. Your light must shine in the sight of men' (Mt 5:14-16). So we pray today as well that we will 'let our light shine', that we will be an example to our children in the way we live and practise our faith. When you think of it – Mary and Joseph presented to God more than five shekels, a pair of turtle doves and even the baby Jesus. They presented themselves, their own lives, their willingness to do his will. It was a characteristic of both of them, their combined, common achievement. Wouldn't it be a lovely thing at this presentation time if we were to do the same! Present arms, the soldiers say. The call to the Christian is to 'present lives'.

Note
1. *Glenstal Bible Missal*, HarperCollins, 1983, p. 1370

THESE MIGHT HELP TOO

Carrying on the Work

Jer 1:4-9; Acts 13:46-49; Lk 10:1-12, 17-20

I always feel on Patrick's Day that what we tend to get in Church is the repetition that kills. The same old story: Patrick's birth in Britain; his capture as a young boy; his shepherding on Sliabh Mish; his escape from slavery; his response to the call of the Irish; his return as priest and bishop; his footprints all over the country; his impact on our people in terms of faith. I'm not saying it isn't true – I'm just wondering how deeply it penetrates or whether Patrick has anything to say to you and me in modern times. Or to put it another way: having heard the biographical details over and over again, do we know anything at all about the inner man? Does this heroic figure have a relevant message for the ordinary person? Let's see!

Near the end of his life, Patrick wrote his autobiography, known to us as *The Confession*. It gives us an insight into his mind and heart. He was a burdened man, a man who was always struggling, a man who was very conscious of his own limitations, especially his sinfulness, and who never thought of himself as a saint at all. The first line of his *Confession* says: 'I am Patrick, a sinner – unlettered – the least of all the faithful and held in contempt by many.' When he came back to Ireland as a missionary he was burdened by loneliness too. He found the going very tough. He was a man in exile. He would never go home again! He said he was lonely, that his mission was very dangerous, that he was betrayed by a close friend, falsely accused of taking money from his converts, that even his own family misunderstood him and, to cap it all, that he was robbed of whatever he had and thrown into prison. So this man was no statue on a plinth or an icon on a pedestal. Here was a man of flesh and blood, deeply enmeshed in the rough and tumble of life. In that way he was one of ourselves – only more so in some ways. Another me, or another you.

What kept him going? Well, first of all, he was very conscious of God's mercy. He talks about it over and over. He never lost faith in that. He says in *The Confession* for instance that 'his littleness was placed among strangers' (in Ireland of course), that the Lord made him aware of his sins, 'had mercy on his youth and ignorance' and 'guarded and comforted him as would a father his son'. Secondly, Patrick was a great man to pray. 'I used to pray many times a day,' he wrote, 'as many as a hundred times – and in the night nearly as often.' He seemed to be in constant contact or rather in constant communion with his God. Thirdly, he felt that his life was hostage to the Holy Spirit, in the sense that the Spirit was his guide and that he must respond to the promptings of the Spirit in everything he did. For instance, he says that he would 'love to go to his country and his parents' and to see the faces of his fellow Christians in Gaul, but is 'bound by the Spirit who gives evidence against me if I do this, telling me that I shall be guilty!' We often think ourselves that the Holy Spirit gives us the advantage of the wind – that we always have wind at our backs if we respond to his promptings. Patrick realised that being obedient to the Spirit meant having the wind in your face at times too and being prepared to make costly personal sacrifices for the sake of the Gospel. Fourthly and finally, what Patrick felt most of all was that he was loved, blessed and called by God to carry on his mission at that particular time in Irish history.[1] The voice of the Irish was also the will of the Lord. 'The Lord gave to them,' Patrick says, 'according to their cry.' So that's the one I'd pick out for you and for me: that we are loved, blessed and called by God to carry on his mission at this particular time in Irish history. So let's get it into our heads – and maybe it will make a difference – that no matter how unworthy or sinful we may feel ourselves to be,

THESE MIGHT HELP TOO

we are loved, blessed and called by God to carry on his mission at this challenging time in our history. We are perfectly entitled on St Patrick's Day to celebrate our Irishness, to rejoice in our achievements as a people, to ensure especially that our children enjoy the freedom of the streets and become gradually more aware of the richness of their inheritance. Our celebrations, however, will never have the comprehensiveness that they should if the Gospel gets lost in the greenery. In the wearing of the shamrock there should always be a consciousness of the vine! A pity if a plant that of its nature is meant to spread should be smothered by another. Death not so much by asphyxiation as inattention. The need for green fingers of the Gospel kind. The deepest significance of Patrick's Day lies not in the parade but in the purpose – God's purpose – that Patrick started something in Ireland that yourself and myself are meant to carry on.

Note

1. Christopher O'Donnell OCarm, *St Patrick – Spirit and Prayer*, McCrimmon Publishing Co. Ltd, 2002.

Relationship in Unity

Prov 8:22-31; Rom 5:1-5; Jn 16:12-15

Jim and Angela were always together. Because I was young at the time, it always struck me as wonderful, but strange. The problem was that they were married. And married couples weren't supposed to behave like that. In the public arena, married couples tended to stay apart. They might go for a walk together, or go to a dance, or bring the baby out in the pram (in which case the man definitely wouldn't push it) but apart from these occasional adventures, in public they kept a careful distance from one another. As everybody knows, it was the age of reticence. In public, married people gave pecks instead of kisses and married women had no first names at all. Jim and Angela were different, not that they were more demonstrative than other couples – they weren't! What made them so different is that one never went anywhere without the other. They were always together. And although they never said a word about it themselves, their being together spoke eloquently of relationship and unity. They were happy together, obviously, and very much in love.

Jim and Angela would be amazed that anyone would choose their marriage as a route into the mystery of the Trinity. And a very humble route it is – as they'd be the first to acknowledge. But it is not an entirely inappropriate route, because the Trinity is all about relationship and unity too or, if you prefer, relationship in unity. And rather than spend the time wondering how there could be three divine persons in one God, far better to reflect for a moment or two on the closeness, highlighted in scripture, between Father, Son and Holy Spirit.

One of the most striking things about Jesus in the Gospels is the loving way in which he spoke about the

Father. I suppose the fact of the matter is that no father and son were ever as close, seeing that all the closeness in the world has its origins in God. It is in John's Gospel that the love of Jesus for the Father is most often expressed. 'Do you not believe,' he says to his disciples, 'that I am in the Father and the Father is in me?' (Jn 14:10). They had better believe it, because he had already told them earlier in John's Gospel that the 'one who sent him was with him' (Jn 8:19) and that the Father and himself were one (Jn 10:30). The depth of Christ's love was really tested in the Garden of Gethsemane when his suffering was so intense that he hoped his Father might spare him (Mt 26:39). His love survived the test. It was too trusting in its nature to fall apart. It would be the Father's will that would prevail, not his own. He gave, on the cross, the fullest possible proof of that love, when he said, 'Father, into your hands I commit my spirit' (Lk 23:46). On the evidence of the Gospels, Jesus didn't talk as much about the Holy Spirit. But he said enough. And what he said was highly significant. One quotation from John illustrates the point: 'But the Advocate the Holy Spirit, whom the Father will send in my name, will teach you everything and remind you of all I have said to you' (Jn 14:26). The Spirit would be sent by the Father in Christ's name. The three are working together in harmony, as one would expect. If we don't find relationship in unity in the Trinity, where are we to find it? John Wesley once made the remark that in a room with three candles you only have one light. In the trinity of persons in heaven you only have one love.

When it comes to relationships or loving one another, I doubt if any of us has any ambition to outperform the Trinity. We know our limitations. It's very unlikely, to put it mildly, that the love of Father, Son and Spirit could be reproduced on earth. But we could take our cue from them and need to take our cue from them, not least within the family. The Trinity is God's inner life. The family is ours. There is no such thing as the perfect family. We all know that. And there is no such thing as the inoculated family. Trouble is not discriminating. It spreads itself comprehensively, if not evenly, amongst us all. At the same time, a home, by and large, ought to be a place of relaxation and peace – where we find the rest we need after a day's work and the energy to face another. I know people who hate going home in the evening, very often because one member of the family makes life unpleasant or even impossible for everybody else. One person's mood is everybody else's misery. One person's self-indulgence is everybody else's cross. It doesn't have to be that way. It wasn't that way with Jim and Angela.

If you happen to be the guilty party, please make a resolution to acknowledge that and to bring the misery to an end. It can be done with genuine goodwill and with the help we all need from above. Please let a beginning be made, this very day, in the name of the Father and of the Son and of the Holy Spirit. Amen.

Friendship with Christ

Gen 14:18-20; 1 Cor 11:23-26; Lk 9:11-17

I've been at six funerals and one wedding in the past few weeks. Even allowing for the randomness of that proportion, it does suggest that death is more dominant than matrimony. In some of these cases, people died without warning. What characterised their going was the unexpectancy. The frequency with which death takes its toll on us and the almost casual nature of its intervention have led me to reflect that life is an ordinary day, followed by an ordinary day and then by the day on which you die. Death is just a sudden stillness. One has to look very closely sometimes to make sure that it's there at all. It is not preceded by a flourish of trumpets or accompanied in nature by a rolling of thunder as deaths in literature sometimes are. It just happens to people – almost apologetically – at an undetermined time while the traffic outside speeds heedlessly by. A short time ago three brothers worked together on a particular project in this parish. Two of them have since died. They were so dependable in their coming to work, so meticulous in the doing of it, that one expected them to go on forever. Surely even death would be helpless in the face of their combined professionalism? It wasn't, and it got there before its time.

What has made life worthwhile for me so far has been love for my parents or, more especially, their love for me; the continuing experience of love within my family; the friendships that mean so much to me; the work that I do every day; and, because we are only passing through and death is so commonplace, the conviction that the Lord is walking with us and leading us beyond the grave to God. *Corpus Christi* means 'Body of Christ'. The feast, by way of the traditional *Corpus Christi* procession, puts special emphasis on Our Lord's presence in the Blessed Sacrament as our companion and friend. If he weren't with us we'd be journeying into the sand. Jesus Christ is not just an historical character. He's a living presence – a risen Saviour in our midst. Today's feast reminds us to take him to our hearts – to be conscious of him, to rely on him, to lean on him, to draw hope from him. Is he really our companion on the journey? If not, aren't we missing out on an awful lot? Where will we find better a friend in life and an ally in death? Samuel Johnson said the following and it's worth noting: 'If a man does not make new acquaintances as he advances through life, he will soon find himself alone; one should keep his friendships in constant repair!'[1] The main friendship we need to keep in constant repair is our friendship with Christ.

Is that all that's to it then? A personal, almost cosy friendship with Christ that will help to sustain us in this life and ensure our salvation in the next? Is that all there is to it? No! Any relationship we have with Our Lord will have to include his people. That much is made very clear in the Gospel and in the second reading. Our Lord multiplied the loaves and fishes in today's Gospel, not to feed his own ego, but because he wanted to feed the people. He gave all of us a headline for our attitude to the hungry when he said to his disciples, 'Give them something to eat yourselves' (Lk 9:13). Since the multiplication of the loaves is a prelude to the institution of the Eucharist, the clear implication is that the Eucharist itself requires us to care for the starving. The language used in the miracle of multiplication is the very same language that Jesus used at the Last Supper and at the supper in Emmaus. He 'took', he 'blessed', he 'broke', he 'gave'.[2] We receive a double message: the body of Christ is something we receive but the body is also out there in the form of needy people.

St Paul reinforces that message in the second reading. It's hard to believe it now, but in Paul's time some of the

THESE MIGHT HELP TOO

richer Corinthian Christians were coming to celebrate the Eucharist with plenty of food and drink for themselves and in the very act of celebration refusing to share it with their poorer Christian neighbours. What was meant to be a common meal had become for some a gluttonous and divisive indulgence. Paul is reminding them that the Last Supper was sacrificial. Jesus gave his body and blood out of love for his brothers and sisters. 'This is my body which is for you … do this as a memorial of me' (1 Cor 11:25). The Eucharist was motivated by love and challenges us to love. If there are starving people in the world – and there are – and if we have more than we need – and we don't share with them – we are not quite as bad as the richer Corinthians perhaps, but we do share their attitude. We are not conscious enough of contradiction. I said earlier that life is an ordinary day, followed by an ordinary day and then by the day on which you die. In the developing world, the day on which you die comes much sooner, not just for thousands, but for millions of people. If our indifference to their need contributes to that – and it does – how in God's name can we claim to have a genuine friendship with Christ? He did say, I know, 'Come to me, all you who labour and are overburdened and I will give you rest' (Mt 11:28). That's one side of it. But he also said in today's Gospel, 'Give them something to eat yourselves'.

Notes
1. Anthony P. Castle, *Quotes and Anecdotes: The Essential Reference for Preachers and Teachers*, Kevin Mayhew, 1995, p. 30.
2. Raymond Brown, *The Jerome Biblical Commentary*, Prentice Hall, 1968, p. 141.

Mary's Assumption – Our Assurance

Apoc 11:19, 12:1-6, 10; 1 Cor 15:20-26; Lk 1:39-56

One thing Gertie had never discovered about her neighbour Mary was her age. Even though they had become great friends since Gertie married into the parish, they had never become friendly enough for the disclosure of such intimacies. Tea, Gertie could borrow in an emergency, and never be short of sugar, but age was a commodity that was kept well out of reach on the top shelf. It was very frustrating to know practically everything about your neighbour except her date of birth. Mary, as fate would have it, was the first of the two women to die. Although her passing came as an awful shock to Gertie, it did present her with the opportunity to find out in death what she had failed to find out in life. Annie Kate, Mary's oldest sister, would surely have the answer. 'And what age was poor Mary?' Gertie wondered innocently. 'Oh, she is Mary with a good while now,' Annie Kate told her solemnly. 'She is Mary with a good while now.' It was a tradition in the family obviously to give nothing away. No website for that household!

Although we have no written references in the early Church to the Assumption of Mary, she is 'Mary assumed into heaven for a good while now'. We cannot say precisely what year the title was first given to her. What we can say with certainty is that the Assumption of Mary has been part of the Church's faith for a very long time. If the presence of the Holy Spirit in the Church means anything at all, then something so widely taught and believed over such a long period must have its ultimate source in the womb of revelation. The Church exults in the Assumption not because it is her invention but because it is her inheritance.

What she receives, she celebrates. In the second half of the sixth century (probably) a Palestinian bishop called Theoteknos was giving joyful expression to the mind of the Church when he said, 'It was fitting that Mary's God-bearing body should be raised up to heaven in glory with her soul' (Encomium 9). The Church of the middle ages was in jubilant agreement with all that. Church after Church was dedicated to the Assumption. In England alone the number was forty-five. Seventeen of these were in the Oxford district. One of the seventeen was so 'taken up' with Our Lady that it had a society attached for the singular purpose of 'honouring God, St Mary and the Festival of the Assumption'. Another of the seventeen not to be outdone, and with an instinct for twinning, was dedicated with delight to 'the Ascension of Our Lord and the Assumption of Our Lady'.[1] By the middle of the twentieth century, devotion to the Assumption had gained so much momentum that when the Holy Father consulted the bishops of the world as to the wisdom of defining the doctrine, the vote in its favour was practically unanimous. Consequently, in 1950, his holiness Pope Pius XII proclaimed it as an article of the Catholic faith that at the end of her earthly life Mary was taken up into heaven body and soul.

What was the compelling reason for Mary's Assumption? Why wasn't her body left to decay in the earth like the bodies of the rest of us? Maybe we have the beginnings of an answer in what St Paul has to say in the second reading. 'Just as all men die in Adam,' he says, 'so all men will be brought to life in Christ, but all in their proper order' (1 Cor 15:22-23). Now, if it were left to you to arrange that order, who would you put first? Who else but Mary? Who amongst us has a better claim? Which of us wants to take precedence over the Mother of God? And if we happen to know our place, God surely knows Mary's. If at the Annunciation, for instance, Mary didn't leave him waiting, was he likely to leave her? Leave a gap between her dying and her glorification in heaven. And can we not see in Christ's Ascension the logic of her Assumption? If she followed in his footsteps shouldn't she be hard on his heels? Since she played such an important part in his mission, since their lives were so closely linked, shouldn't their destinies be linked as well?

And finally, have we not reason to see in Mary's Assumption, if not the logic, at least the promise of our own? Surely where the mother has gone, the children can hope to follow? The fact that Mary is the first of the redeemed, that a human being like ourselves is already secure in heaven, that what makes all of us die can never kill Mary, is the one part of the Church's teaching that, after the Resurrection, gives me the greatest hope. The Feast of the Assumption is not just a feast. What it is, more than anything else, is an assurance. If Mary is assumed into heaven for a good while now – and she is – then with God's help and Mary's intercession, all of us will get to heaven for a good while too.

Note

1. See Francis Drake in Kevin McNamara (ed.), *Mother of the Redeemer*, M.H. Gill & Son, 1959, p. 187.

THESE MIGHT HELP TOO

The Triumph of the Cross

Num 21:4-9; Phil 2:6-11; Jn 3:13-17

One of the things that is very securely established about Jesus of Nazareth is that he was put to death on a cross. Historians are so sure of this that they can almost put a date on it. The date is probably 7 April AD 30. I say probably – the date is, of course, disputed. The death itself is not.

In the years before Christ was born, there was a huge revolt by the slaves in Italy led by a man called Spartacus. Would you believe that, at one stage, he controlled the whole of Southern Italy with a slave army 90,000 strong! When they had defeated them in battle, the Romans crucified as many of the survivors as they could lay their hands on. That's what crucifixion was for – slaves and rebels! Crucifixion was such a disgraceful and ignominious death that Roman citizens were never crucified. It was such a degrading death that the Roman writer Cicero said: 'The idea of the cross should never come near the bodies of Roman citizens; it should never pass through their thoughts, their eyes or ears.' Jesus was executed by the Romans as a political rebel. That's why they attached to the cross the inscription, 'King of the Jews'. By crucifying him they were extinguishing the lowest form of life in their society. When the sun went down on him on Good Friday evening, it went down on his disgrace.

Look at the crucifix. It is no longer a symbol of disgrace but a symbol we revere and love. We have it on the altar for the purpose of veneration. We carried it in procession at the beginning of mass to give it prominence and recognition. It's the one object we kiss in church in the course of the whole year. The cross is the sign we make on the foreheads of our babies at Baptism when we claim them for Christ; it's the sign confirming that our sins are forgiven in the Sacrament of Reconciliation; it's the object we place in the hands of our loved ones when they are dying. It's the one religious object that, I hope, all of us have in our homes. And the cross is the object we look to for hope and encouragement when we are carrying our own. It's the cross more than any other object or sign that has come to dominate and even define our lives. 'The cross of Christ about us' we say, and all about us it is. We are the King of Friday's men and women under the sign of the cross.

The reason that the cross has come to dominate our lives is that it is the manifestation of God's love for us and the instrument of our salvation. 'God loved the world so much that he gave his only Son so that everyone who believes in him may not be lost but may have eternal life' (Jn 3:16). Our Lord offered his life for our salvation, not to appease an angry God but to win back a wayward people; to make a new covenant with God that was sealed with his blood. St Paul talked about it in today's second reading. 'He emptied himself, to assume the condition of a slave. He was humbler yet even to accepting death, death on a cross' (Phil 2:7-8). The whole thing was foretold by the prophet Isaiah in the Song of the Suffering Servant. 'Ours were the sufferings he bore; ours the sorrows he carried. He was pierced through for our faults – crushed for our sins – through his wounds we are healed!' (Is 53:4-5). Christ's death on the cross was a saving event, saving us from the slavery of sin, from the consequences of man's disobedience. It was a redemptive death that reunited people with God. We say on Good Friday, 'This is the wood of the cross on which hung the Saviour of the world. Come let us adore'.

Is there any other reason why the cross has come to dominate and define our lives? Oh yes, there is. When Our Lord died on Good Friday, some of his disciples took the body down and laid it in a tomb. The final courtesy. As the sun went down that evening, if they had looked at it, they would have seen the cross silhouetted against the skyline – a dark and bleak reminder of the horrible death that had been inflicted on their leader and a reminder too of a mission that had failed. The day belonged to death and the night was closing in on it. But if they had seen the sun come up on Easter Sunday morning, they would have seen its rays glinting off the cross, changing its colour and complexion. They would have seen the light of the Resurrection transform the entire history of the cross and give it a meaning and a future it never had before. The cross lives now in reflected light. The light of the Resurrection. If Christ had not risen, the cross would have remained only a cross, a symbol of disgrace and defeat, but because he did rise from the dead it has become for the world a symbol of celebration and victory. Today, all over the world the Church is rejoicing in that victory so we rejoice too as we say together, 'Dying you destroyed our death. Rising you restored our life. Lord Jesus come in glory'.

One Man's Story

It was the evening of the ninth of May, 1946. A young priest called Fr Luke Lynch would be leaving for China early the following morning. He was heading off on his first assignment as a missionary. His neighbours in the parish of Moynalty, Co. Meath came in to say goodbye. This leave-taking wasn't easy for him because he'd be gone for at least ten years. Hardest of all would be leaving his father and mother who were both nearly seventy years of age and who, in all probability, would never see him again. The last of the neighbours left about midnight. Fr Luke walked with them to the gate. When he returned to the house his brothers and sisters had gone to bed. His father and mother were sitting at the fire in complete silence. There wasn't much any of them could say that would ease the pain. Both parents were paying an awful price for the vocation of their son. So was the young man himself. Years later, Fr Luke was to write in his autobiography that when he stood before God in judgement, he hoped that no matter what sins he had committed, full account would be taken of the sacrifice he'd had to make on that night.

Fr Lynch travelled by ferry from Dun Laoghire to Liverpool and from there by ship to Shanghai. The voyage took four and a half months. Talk about a slow boat to China. After spending a number of months in a language school in Huchow he was appointed as a curate in an entirely rural parish with not a shop within four miles. No chance of an ice-cream there – and an ice-cream would have been very welcome because the temperature was 102 degrees Fahrenheit in the shade, though it did come down to 97 degrees at night. It was a relatively easy parish in that the two out-stations were only six and four miles away. By Chinese standards he didn't have far to walk in and out. There were the usual things: masses, confessions, weddings, funerals and so forth. The one thing that made him less lonely than he might otherwise be was that at lunch and tea-time the walls of his living room would be lined with visitors watching him eat and plying him with questions – a Chinese custom, which, thanks be to God, we don't have in this country.

A few years later – when his health gave cause for concern – Fr Lynch was moved to a city parish in Shanghai. He was barely settled in when he woke up one May morning in 1949 to the sound of martial music on the radio and the news that the Communists had taken over in China from the Nationalist leader, Chiang Kai Shek. In a campaign against 'spies', 10,000 people were arrested in *one night* in Shanghai. The sound of the execution wagon going through the streets became a familiar and frightening reality and there was so much harassment and persecution of those who weren't Communist that protest suicides – people jumping to their deaths from high buildings – became a daily occurrence. The persecuted sought refuge in oblivion and hoped their dying would bring new life to others.

One man for whom the protests didn't bring new life was the Bishop of Shanghai, a man called Kung. Bishop Kung was the first Chinese Bishop of Shanghai. Prior to that the city's bishop had always been a French Jesuit. From 1951 onwards, he was under intense pressure to admit Communist teachers to his schools, to hand over hospital sisters accused of killing babies by the thousands and then to break completely with Rome. Because he resisted the pressure for several years – and resolutely refused to do any of these things – he was arrested in 1955. He was subjected to torture for three months and when his gaolors believed he was ready to break and make a public confession they arranged for a public trial in a large square in front of the biggest Catholic Church in Shanghai. In the square 5,000 Catholics were rounded up and ordered to shout in the voice of the people for the bishop's execution. The bishop himself was standing, in his underwear, on a floodlit platform, his hands tied behind his back, his chin almost touching his chest. When the moment of acute humiliation had come he was pushed towards the microphone and ordered to 'Confess – Confess'. There was a slogan in China at the time – on buses, on hoardings all over the place. 'Long live Mao Tse-tung.' Bishop Kung shuffled to the microphone, straightened himself up and shouted three times: 'Long live Christ the King.' The crowds took up the chant – the persecutors lost their nerve and, instead of the firing squad, the Bishop faced thirty years of internment in a labour camp. He was released in 1985. In 1991 Pope John Paul created twenty-two new cardinals. If you were watching the ceremony on TV the last man up to greet the Pope was Cardinal Kung of Shanghai.

I tell you all this because Fr Luke Lynch worked with us for a few years in the diocese of Tuam. I'm telling you, more so, because what I've said so far is just a tiny part of one man's experience of mission. It's one small insight into the missionary endeavour. Granted the emphasis so far has been on sacrifice and heroism. I'm not suggesting that every missionary is necessarily heroic. Human beings are far too fragile and complex for that. What I am saying is that there is heroism in our history and we shouldn't easily forget it. Where is our idealism now? Where is our enthusiasm – our passion for spreading the Gospel? The Church to which we belong is essentially missionary. It hasn't been left by Christ but sent by Christ to be a sacrament of salvation for all mankind. 'Go therefore and make disciples of all the nations' (Mt 28:19). If the Church hadn't a message to spread – or rather a person to make known – it would have no reason to be. To be a member of the Church is to be a missionary for Christ. Those who are out on the Missions now are practical people. They ask for three things from us – that we pray for them, offer our sufferings for them and support them financially. The collection for the Missions or the Propagation of the Faith will be in three weeks time. Please think about it in the meantime. And with what you put in the envelope, don't make his face fall – make it shine!

Saints instead of Samhain

Apoc 7:2-4, 9-14; 1 Jn 3:1-3; Mt 5:1-12

Does Halloween strike you as an unusual feast? Do you think it is unusual? It is in the sense that it has a number of features that we don't normally associate with religion. The image of the cat, for instance, and the mask, and the pumpkin, and the bonfire. The bonfire we do somewhat associate with religion – but not the other three. The reason for this difference is that Halloween has pagan roots, a pagan underside. In Ireland and Scotland it goes back to pre-Christian times, to the time of the druids. In those days the Celtic year ended on October 31. So Halloween was the eve of *Samhain* – the eve of November. Now, *Samhain* was a double feast: it was the end of summer and it was a festival of the dead. The dead were believed to come back to their families looking for warmth and food before the winter began. So people used to leave out food for them, as well as storing up food for themselves in the face of the winter. That may explain the variety of foods at Halloween: the apples, the nuts, the barmbrack and so forth. Anyway, the two major points to remember are that this was the end of summer and the festival of the dead.

Halloween was a time for magic too, for trying to foretell the future. People used magic in an effort to discover who would be the first to die (the pumpkin is the image of the skull) and who'd get married to whom (the origin of the ring). It was a time when fairies, witches and goblins roamed the earth to terrify the population. These praeternatural creatures were supposed to steal babies, destroy crops and kill animals. People used to light bonfires, some think to guide the dead home, others, to drive away the witches, others still, to help the sun through the winter.

It was a time to keep your head down and to stay indoors. And when you did, groups of peasants would come knocking at the door looking for food and drink for the evening's festivities. If you didn't treat them, they'd play a trick on you, just as witches and goblins were alleged to do! 'Trick or Treat'! So as I say, the feast has deep pagan roots.

The Church used to have a feast of All Saints in the middle of May. But in the eighth century she thought it better to locate it in the middle of paganism and to move the feast from May 13 to November, as a counterweight to paganism. This put the emphasis on the supernatural rather than the praeternatural, wooing people away from the witches and getting them to focus on the saints. The old word for 'saint' in English is 'hallow'. 'All Hallows' is the older 'All Saints'. 'Een' of course is the shorter version of 'evening'. Halloween is the evening before the feast of saints. When in the eighth century the feast was first moved to November, the saints were the Church's answer to *Samhain*.

The important point to grasp is that they still are. And the fact that they are has to do with today's Gospel (Mt 5:1-12). One of the things that Jesus is doing in this Gospel is enunciating a set of values that would be foundational in the kingdom he was putting in place. The important ones are poverty of spirit, gentleness, forgiveness, a hunger for justice, a passion for peace, a readiness to suffer in his name. They are very much at variance with pagan or worldly values such as pride, vindictiveness, belligerence, aggrandisement and war. But Jesus is doing more than enunciating a set of values. He is describing the kind of people who would be the citizens of his kingdom and who would be the stuff or material out of which saints are made. People like that are the poor in spirit who recognise their own limitations, their need of God and their total dependence on him. They are the gentle ones whose gentleness is based on reverence for others and respect for human life. They are the mournful ones, not because they are gloomy by nature but because they mourn their own weakness, are sorry for their own sins and feel the need of God's comfort. In case we are getting the impression that the citizens of the kingdom have nothing to offer us except bowed shoulders and a gentle embrace, Jesus reminds us in the middle of the 'beatitudes' that they have to be made of robust and resilient stuff as well. They have to be positive, constructive and courageous. They have to be engaged with the world and concerned with the needs of others. They have to be working for justice, struggling for integrity in their own lives, doing everything in their power to bring combatants together in peace. They are the kind of people who build up community and they are the kind of people from whom we have sprung. Although we looked on them only as humans, the people who reared us were saints. We thought saints were only pictures on the walls, but they were all around us on the ground. They were struggling sinners too of course – as all saints are – but they added to their sanctity in the struggle, as all saints do. We remember them now with gratitude and affection. All of us are so deeply in their debt. The magic in their lives had nothing to do with foretelling the future and everything to do with their legacy from the past. May we cherish that legacy, and value it and add to it as best we can, as we celebrate with the Church universal the Feast of All Saints!

Index

discrimination
  on racial and religious grounds
  166–7
  on moral grounds, 193–5
division over Jesus, 180–3

E
Easter
  and appearances, 92, 99
  and the Cross, 247
  and the disciples, 92, 99
  and ignition, 98
  preparing for, 61–3, 64–6
elderly, concern for, 176
Elijah and Jesus, 150–1
Emmaus, Jesus by our side, 101
enemies, love of, 50, 141–2,
  165–7
Epiphany
  Jesus as friend, 52–3, 242
  as Saviour, 53–4
Eucharist
  challenge to love, 242
  Christ's presence, 242
  as sacrifice, 86–7
existence of God
  and God speaking to us, 56–7
  and order in Universe, 55–6
exaltation of Christ, 115–16
Ezekiel and shepherding, 106

F
faith
  of centurion, 147
  factors undermining, 202
  a personal journey, 182–3
  and the problem of evil, 202
family
  division within, 181–2
  hatred between members, 190
  peace in, 40–1, 42–4, 239–40
first fruits given to God, 156
following Jesus, 89, 107–8, 160–1,
  181–3

forgiveness
  and prodigal Son, 73–5
  and the publican, 213
  and the woman in adultery, 76
  and the woman with bad name,
  153–4
  and Zachaeus, 214–16
fortitude, need for, 221
friendship
  with Christ, 241
  need for, 52, 117

G
generosity
  of God, 117
  towards poor, 62, 199
glorification of Jesus, 115
God
  his compassion, 70
  his existence, 55
  his forgiveness, 73, 76, 153,
  213, 214–16
  his love for us, 55
Good Friday, 88
good Samaritan, 165
good shepherd, 73
good steward
  in Gospel, 178
  in life, 177
good word, beneficial effects of,
  144–5
gratitude
  of Mary, 231
  of samaritan, 206
  in our lives, 207, 225

H
Halloween, unusual customs, 254
healing
  of centurion's servant, 146
  of many others, 172
Herod the Great, 49
Holy family, dealing with
  problems, 39, 43

THESE MIGHT HELP TOO

Holy Spirit
  impact on disciples, 120
  in life of Patrick, 236
  role of spirit, 113–14
home, peace in, 40, 42–3
Hopkins, Gerard Manley, 30–1, 188
hospitality, 168–9
humility
  of centurion towards God, 147
  and others, 187–9
  of Mary, 231
  of publican, 213

I
Immaculate Conception, 229
Incarnation, 35, 51
individuals
  God's love for, 194–5
  role of, 91–2
ingratitude of lepers, 205
intercession at God's right hand, 116–17
isolation, experience of, 100, 149

J
Jerusalem
  facing for, 159, 184
  on feast of Passover, 85
Jesus
  and authority, 135
  and birth of, 13, 21, 24, 30, 33, 35
  and the difference in him, 125
  and friendship, 52, 100, 242
  and gentile world, 146
  and healing, 146, 172
  and light, 178–9
  and new teaching, 128, 134
  and people, 125
  and shepherding, 106
  as Son of God, 35, 49
  and temptation, 65–6

John the Baptist, major figure, 16
judgement, preparing for, 14, 189
justice, component of love, 111
joy
  during Advent, 20–1
  in heaven, 74
  of prodigal father, 73–5
  at year's end, 223

K
King, Christ the, 223
kingdom
  citizens of, 255–6
  nature of, 163
  new departure, 140–1
  values of, 139, 255

L
lamb of deliverance, 157
last supper
  institution of Eucharist, 85
leprosy in bible, 205
lent
  and brevity of life, 61
  and preparing for Easter, 61, 64–6
life, making it worthwhile, 241
love
  of enemies, 140, 166
  of family, 239–40
  new commandment, 109

M
marriage in life to come, 217
Martha and Mary, 168
Mary
  and Assumption, 244
  and her humanity, 23, 229
  and Immaculate Conception, 229
  and the Presentation, 232
  and redemption, 245

INDEX 259

THESE MIGHT HELP TOO